CHIN UP BRITAIN

Jenny Eclair has been a stand-up comic since the last millennium and has been around the block more times than is polite to count.

As Team Captain and co-writer (with Judith Holder) of the *Grumpy Old Women Live* shows, she has spent the past five years trying to knock some sense back into society. This book is the definitive guide to living without silliness.

Eclair is also a novelist and playwright, she is on the radio quite a lot and is about to start a petition to get her own afternoon television chat show – fingers crossed, eh!

Eclair has written quite a lot of books including the novels *Camberwell Beauty* and *Having a Lovely Time*. She also co-wrote *Wendy: The Bumper Book of Fun for Women of a Certain Age* with Judith Holder.

She gigs regularly all over the country, but can also be seen in Sainsbury's in South London where she lives (in South London, not in Sainsbury's) with her partner St Geof and their daughter.

Jenny Eclair is fifty years old and trying not to mind. On a more cheerful note, she was recently made an honorary Doctor of Philosophy by Middlesex University – a title she tends to use *ad nauseum* (yes, now she is a Doctor she sometimes talks in Latin).

She is five foot four of dyed blonde hair and glasses.

Grumpy Old Women everywhere say...

CHIN UP BRITAIN

RESTORING
COMMON
SENSE TO THE
NATION

JENNY ECLAIR

(with a bit of help from Judith Holder)

headline

First published in 2010
by HEADLINE PUBLISHING GROUP

1

Cataloguing in Publication Data is available from the British Library

ISBN 978 0 7553 6060 4

Design by Jim Lockwood

Printed and bound in Great Britain by Clays, St Ives plc

Headline's policy is to use papers that are natural, renewable and recyclable products and made from wood grown in sustainable forests. The logging and manufacturing processes are expected to conform to the environmental regulations of the country of origin.

HEADLINE PUBLISHING GROUP
An Hachette UK Company
338 Euston Road
London NW1 3BH

www.headline.co.uk
www.hachette.co.uk

Courtesy of The Advertising Archives: 135; 164. Courtesy of Avalon: 11. Illustration by Beach: 71. Illustration by Mick Brownfield: 3; 121. Josella Colquhoun (Tack-o-rama): 7; 8; 9; 10; 27; 43; 44; 62; 63; 110; 163; 165b; 171. Susannah Henry (knitted breast enhancers): 67. Jim Lockwood: 60, 72, 73, 74, 75, 106t, 109. Press Association: 146. Shutterstock: 53; 54; 76; 102; 128; 155 (both). Emma Stoney (cross-stitch): 112.

INTRODUCTION

THE LITERARY EQUIVALENT OF A MARKS & SPENCER'S MEAL DEAL FOR TWO
(A MAIN, A SIDE, A PUD AND A BOTTLE OF WINE, ALL FOR A TENNER!)

At last a book for right-minded men and women who are fed up with shilly-shallying. As we know, the country has been on its knees (like an arthritic whore) for far too long. We've lost ourselves in mumbo-jumbo, tied ourselves up with red tape and EU gibberish, and the consequences are dire. Look at the state of us: floundering in debt, riddled with STDs and, despite every effort, still failing to win the Eurovision Song Contest.

Chin Up Britain tells it like it is. Part manifesto, part guidebook, part call to arms, this is a book for people who want to see some sense restored to society. If a book could box the ears of a nation, this would be the book to do it.

Are you fed up with being taken for a ride and treated like a mug? Then this is the manual for you. Better than a self-help book, cheaper than therapy, *Chin Up Britain* will fire you up and inspire you to change not only the way you live, but the way the rest of the country lives too. Prepare to unleash your inner bossy boot.

This book will change your life. You might even walk differently. It will make you stride into the future with newly awakened purpose, with vim, vigour and – dare we say? – spunk.

Chin Up Britain is not just a lazy, nostalgic plunder of times gone by; it's a guide to making the future work by restoring some basic manners and using some simple common sense.

And all for under a tenner!

As if I'm going to let you jokers know where I live!

August 2010

Hello, dear reader.

Thanks for buying this, unless of course you're flipping through a copy in your local bookshop (with your big, grubby hands), thinking, Well, I could buy this for cousin Maxine, but then again, why should I bother?

The great thing about the recession is that it's a glorious excuse to cut down on extraneous spending – my mother, for example, has decided that she is going to choose which of her three children she likes the best and, come Christmas, whoever that might be will be rewarded accordingly. Well done, Mum, you tight-fisted old bag. (Oh listen, it's no good me even trying: she's always liked my brother more than me – I don't stand a chance.)

But favouritism is just one way you can have fun in a recession. For other tips, you really need to get your purse out and actually buy this book. Go on – it will save you money in the long run. Of course, stealing a copy is another option, but look around... See that woman in the beige mac? She is a store detective and she is watching you. Go on – buy the damn book.

Contents include invaluable tips on:
* how to tell kids they can't have a PS3: I want never gets
* how to make a party dress out of rubbish
* how to feed a family of four without spending a single penny
* how to make broad beans edible
  and loads more.

Jenny

FORM THE DON'T BE SO SILLY PARTY

The trouble with this country is there is too much silliness. And whose fault is it? Not ours, that's for sure. It's the suits in charge who are to blame. We're talking politicians here. With the possible exception of Obama, we wouldn't trust any of them with a pair of scissors. So let's sack the lot of them. I know they've only been in for two minutes, but we can form a new party, the Don't Be So Silly Party, and recruit some members with a bit of phlegm and spunk (not that kind).

We need people who are courageous, selfless and steadfast, who will thrive on hard work and stride about in a pair of long, baggy shorts with a lot of pockets that flap around in the wind. They will shun molly-coddling and extravagance, and will have no time at all for nonsense or impractical shoes. In other words, they need to be like famous people in times gone by, people like Lord and Lady Baden-Powell, and Sir Douglas Bader, who managed to be upstanding even with no legs.

In order to be elected, our future leaders will have done something properly important or properly difficult and will possibly have suffered the loss of a digit due to frostbite. (That Ben Fogle chap is shaping up quite nicely for the future.)

Or why not give the job to the only people in the country we can trust? Our senior citizens. (Not the very old, obviously. If you've given up the allotment, then running the country might be a bit too much of a hoo-ha.) We're talking the 60- and 70-somethings who are still capable of making a fist and shaking it. Let's hear it for wisdom and experience. Let's hear it for people who have learned from their mistakes. Let's dig out all the retired geography teachers and ex-headgirls and -boys, the captains of golf clubs and really bossy dinner ladies and put them in charge.

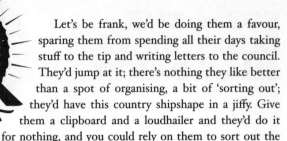

Let's be frank, we'd be doing them a favour, sparing them from spending all their days taking stuff to the tip and writing letters to the council. They'd jump at it; there's nothing they like better than a spot of organising, a bit of 'sorting out'; they'd have this country shipshape in a jiffy. Give them a clipboard and a loudhailer and they'd do it for nothing, and you could rely on them to sort out the important issues, such as slagginess and the appalling way our elderly citizens are treated. For starters, the Don't Be So Silly Party would...

Bring Back Virginity

Back in the old days, people weren't so silly about looks; other things were just as important, like being a nice person or a virgin. Unfortunately, these days no one cares about niceness or virginity. Let's face it, there's no point standing next to Cheryl Cole and saying, 'Yes, but I'm nicer than her and I'm a virgin.'

Obviously we need to bring back some old-fashioned values regarding looks. Girls need to stop wasting valuable time and energy on silly treatments and expensive cosmetics and simply start washing their faces in soap and water and wearing Alice bands. Hoorah – a whole generation of young girls looking as plain as pikestaffs, which leaves us middle-aged women feeling much happier with our lot. What we want is for girls to look more like Sunday-school teachers than pole-dancers. Mind you, I bet there's a call for pole-dancers who look like Sunday-school teachers. Oh God, now look what I've started.

Keep Children As Children

Another thing we need to do pronto is to nip the sexualisation of young women in the bud. Children should be children for much longer. Therefore we should pass a law saying that girls can only wear dresses with smocking on the chest and flat buckle shoes until they are eighteen. They should also wear vests, which should be tucked into their pants, pants that should contain a hanky tucked into the knicker leg. Boys will wear long, grey shorts. This combination of short trousers and smocking will reduce the number of teen pregnancies in no time at all. I have no idea why someone hasn't thought of this before.

Once teen pregnancies have plummeted, the Don't Be So Silly Party would...

Ban Ageism

It's high time people got their priorities right: in recent years there has been far too much emphasis on youth and good looks, which is why stupid, pretty girls are valued more than middle-aged old bags. Well, this has got to stop. We're sick of young girls who think they're it. We're fed up with all those silly girls who are nothing more than seven stone of fake tan in a pair of Ugg boots. DAMN THEM AND THEIR STUPID EMPTY BRAINS.

It's the people who run the telly channels who need to be put up against the wall and shot. Ageism is their fault, so it's time they started making amends. Bring back ancient newscasters, complete with colostomy bags, and put them safely behind their desks, where they can read the news wearing their slippers.

Instead of all those young floozies, why don't they employ middle-aged weathergirls? OK, so they might get a bit muddled up trying to tell their low pressures from their isobars, but that's varifocals for you. As for the fact that 'It might be minus nine in Aberdeen, but it's ever so hot in the studio, what with the lights, and does anyone mind if we just stop for a bit while I take my cardie off?' Does it really matter? We'll all be 50 one day, unless of course you don't think you can hack it and decide to put a bullet through your brain.

VOTE DON'T BE SO SILLY – YOU KNOW IT MAKES SENSE.

The New Don't Be So Silly Party Manifesto

Ⓠ An annual overdue-library-book amnesty day – on this special day forgetful people can take back their overdue library books without running the risk of a fine or a prison sentence.

Ⓠ A £50 cap on a standard-class rail ticket – if train fares weren't so expensive, then maybe people would use them more often.

Ⓠ Litter louts will be forced to eat the litter they have dropped.

Ⓠ A fully paid day off work for anyone celebrating their 50th birthday and the morning off the next day should they have 'a bit of a head'.

Ⓠ The introduction of Jane – a women's telly channel to rival boys'-own telly channel Dave; it's only fair.

Ⓠ Banks and post offices to supply plentiful working biros on all counters – you want us to fill in your silly forms, then the least you can do is meet us halfway.

Ⓠ Compulsory Cycling Proficiency tests for anyone wanting to ride a bike and the signing of a legal pledge not to ride on pavements or through red traffic lights.

Ⓠ The legal drinking age to be raised to 21 – this will mean kids start drinking at eighteen rather than fifteen.

Ⓠ All judges on talent shows to be constructive in their criticism. Should they be rude to a contestant, said contestant should automatically receive ten bonus points – how on earth can we stop bullying in our schools when it's positively encouraged on prime-time television?

Add your own ideas here and maybe one day you could be a member of the Don't Be So Silly government!

_____

_____

_____

STOP THE ROT

It was Whitney Houston who once sang, 'I believe that children are our future,' and she might well be right! The new Don't Be So Silly Party can focus on the two qualities that have gone missing in our society: discipline and its other half, respect. So much rot has set in and it has spread so far that the only way to turn this round is to concentrate on the next generation. To stop the rot spreading any further we need to look at why things went wrong in the first place.

In times gone by, before Sky+, and when blackberries were things that went into crumbles, children were seen and not heard; they were put out in their pram to harden off in the frost. When they were a bit older and weren't crying, they got some Plasticine on newspaper on the kitchen table and learned to cut out shapes with special blunt scissors while being supervised at all times.

Then what happened? Women got it into their heads that they wanted careers as well as babies.

They liked buying shoes and wearing a lot of make-up instead of pushing a carpet cleaner around in a pinny. Hence the trouble started... Working mothers who felt guilty about being at work all day and came home too knackered to do anything more than drink Chardonnay allowed their children to run amok, please themselves and become little monsters that grew up to be the teenagers from hell.

This has to stop. It's time we turned the tide of kiddie tyranny and stopped giving them the impression that life is all about doing as you please – because it's not.

PUTTING THE NEXT GENERATION ON THE COLLECTIVE NAUGHTY STEP

1) Children should once again be taught to sit still, shut up and do as they're told.

2) The under-twelves should not be on first-name terms with adults – 'It's "Mrs Jones" to you, young lady.'

3) Children will no longer be given choices at mealtimes. Eating at home is not the same as eating in a restaurant; you do not get a menu! Cabbage will be back in a very big way.

4) Schools should teach children practical skills – needlework, domestic science and woodwork will once again be compulsory. It may have taken us three terms to make a gingham apron but at least now we can take up a hem without using silly sticky iron tape or having to pay the dry-cleaner to do it for us.

5) Teenagers should be taught good old-fashioned qualities such as cushion-plumping and not sitting down until everything is done – the kind of qualities that we need in a crisis.

6) University places should only be given to students willing to learn social as well as academic skills. What's the point in churning out millions of 21-year-old humanities graduates who can't answer a phone nicely or write a letter?

7) Boys should be encouraged to refind their masculinity and stop being lily-livered, limp, lazy gits who can't pull their trousers up properly or read a map.

8) Youths who refuse to stand up for old ladies on the bus will be thrown off the vehicle.

9) Pocket money will be index-linked to household chores and won't go up until interest rates do.

> **Young people need to realise that their elders have skills and wisdom that are worth passing down the generations and that sneering at them and calling them saddos is not on.**

OTHER SKILLS WE NEED TO TEACH THE NEXT GENERATION

- how to take something back to Debenhams when you've already worn it for a whole summer
- stealing hotel freebies without getting caught
- buttering bread without making a mess
- bargain-hunting
- a work ethic
- using the Yellow Pages
- using a dictionary
- shoe-polishing
- gravy-making without granules.

> **Only when all these rules have been absorbed into the mainstream will we once again have a civilised society.**

THE SKINFLINT'S CALENDAR

HOW TO SAVE MONEY THROUGHOUT THE YEAR

Don't just chuck away those Christmas cards; keep them – you can make gift tags out of them. Just cut round the nice pictures with crimping scissors – yes, you are turning into your mum and there's nothing wrong with that. Obviously you might have to fork out for a pair of crimping scissors, but think of them as an investment rather than an extravagance. You can spend days on end cutting round a little red robin on a gatepost and then punching a hole with your hole-punch. It's better than going on a meditation week in Turkey and a whole lot cheaper.

Make your New Year's resolutions and bet yourself 50 quid that you'll keep them for at least a month. Make sure you make 'em nice and easy – for example, go for resolutions such as 'I am never going to be nice to my husband again' or 'I am never, ever going to remember to have my bag for life on me when I go to the supermarket' and – bingo! – that 50 quid is yours, all yours. See – you're on a winning streak already!

Do not join a gym. This will be your biggest saving this year, as most gym memberships cost around £400. Use this saved money to go on holiday later in the year. OK, so you might look rubbish in your bikini, but at least you'll be somewhere hot. Who's the winner? You are.

Buy next Christmas's wrapping paper, cards and so on right now, while they are half-price. Timing is crucial when it comes to

14

saving money. Mind you, so is finding somewhere to keep this stuff where it's not going to get all crumpled and battered – and don't forget to put a note in your diary reminding yourself that you have bought all this crap, otherwise come December you will have forgotten – you idiot. (PS This will only work if you remember to look in your diary – you might need to put a note on the bathroom mirror to tell you do that. On the other hand, you might have stopped looking in the bathroom mirror for fear of cardiac arrest, in which case we can't really offer much help.)

Buy a really cheap diary from last year and spend a couple of afternoons simply changing the dates to match this year's.

Put your name down for an allotment. With any luck, you'll get one before you are physically incapable of pushing a wheelbarrow.

Cull your friends. Have a really good look at the names in your mobile-phone contacts list. Do you really want to know some of these people? Think friend, or sponger? Separate the wheat from the chaff. You will save a fortune not having to lend them fivers or buy them drinks (because their boyfriend just dumped them again) or meet up for pizzas you don't really want in places you always thought were a rip-off. Remember, the average birthday card in the shops is £2.50. Cut ten friends out of your life and you will save £25 on greetings cards alone (never mind the stamps).

Ignore Valentine's Day. It's a stupid commercial rip-off, and anyway, you haven't got a boyfriend/girlfriend.

Hide £5 in the pocket of a pair of summer shorts. The glee you will feel when you find this fiver will be worth at least a tenner. Note: just make sure you don't put on so much weight that you can't fit into the shorts and you end up giving them (and the fiver) to a charity shop. Also, the British summer is so unpredictable that it could be years until it's nice enough for shorts. Risky.

Get your children to make friends with a kid who has really wealthy parents. With any luck they will have a gîte in the Dordogne. Bingo – that's your summer holiday sorted.

Pretend it's your birthday at work. Your colleagues are bound to take you out for lunch. They might even have a whip round and buy you a nice present, so drop massive hints about what you'd like in advance. Make sure you leave the job before your real birthday comes along. By the same token, if someone's birthday is coming up and they've dropped hints about an expensive after-work meal they're planning for everyone, make sure you are on an away-day in Nuneaton, or take a sickie.

Don't buy any Easter eggs; just tell everyone you have and then pretend to have hidden them in really tricky-to-find places – obviously no one will find them because they don't exist.

Keep your eyes peeled for umbrellas that people leave on the bus. Collect as many as you can and with any luck you will never have to buy an umbrella again.

Book a train ticket to somewhere you might like to visit – maybe Bath? As long as you book your train ticket three months in advance, it will hardly cost you anything. All you need to do is remember to go when the time comes.

Volunteer to be a guinea pig for medical science. This can have disastrous consequences, but on the other hand, you will get some cash.
Sue the NHS for mucking about with you. You never wanted to be a guinea pig really and now you've got whiskers.

Look out for 'clouts that have been cast before May is out'; this is the time to gather cardigans and scarves that have been left lying around on park benches because the sun came out for 20 seconds. Last year I found a really nice apple-green cashmere sweater in Dulwich Park.

Get a job as a Wimbledon ballboy or -girl. The money will be rubbish, but you can sell the balls that they shoved down their pants for at least a fiver each.

Fake-tan your legs DIY style, literally. Nip down to your nearest hardware store and buy some Ronseal wood stain. Choose the colour that most closely matches the skin tone you fancy. Apply a layer of wood varnish for a longer-lasting summer glow.

Grown out of last year's swimming costume? Don't pay for a new one; just book your holiday on a naturist resort.

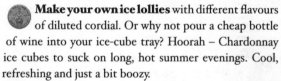

Make your own ice lollies with different flavours of diluted cordial. Or why not pour a cheap bottle of wine into your ice-cube tray? Hoorah – Chardonnay ice cubes to suck on long, hot summer evenings. Cool, refreshing and just a bit boozy.

Pretend to have been kidnapped and demand a ransom from your nearest and dearest. You don't need to ask for very much; a couple of hundred quid added to what you saved by not joining a gym back in January will buy you a couple of weeks somewhere nice and sunny, and while we're on the subject of holidays...

Don't forget to go on that day trip to Bath that you booked three months ago.

Remember to steal toilet rolls wherever you go. For some reason, people often don't lock up their loo rolls; you can find them lying around in public toilets of all description. There should never be any need to buy your own toilet roll. Always carry a large Mulberry handbag for this very reason. People who carry Mulberry handbags are officially above suspicion.*

----

* Don't try and nick the very big toilet rolls they have in motorway service stations – anything that can't easily fit into your handbag or under your jumper is silly.

Experience Scandinavia on the cheap: spend August bank-holiday Monday in Ikea. Treat yourself to some meatballs and hang the expense. This will have the added advantage of giving you the opportunity to bag some brown paper, bubble wrap and string from the counter just beyond the tills before you get to the hot dogs... You haven't bought anything that needs wrapping, but that's your stationery cupboard stocked up nicely. A double whammy.

Do not buy a new car. Well done – you have just saved £25,000. Spend what you like for the rest of the month – you've sacrificed enough.

Pretend to be a tortoise and go into hibernation. All you need is a cardboard box to curl up in. Sleeping is the cheapest way to live. Note: you will need either a very large airing cupboard or an accessible loft.

Pretend to be a new teacher in your local comprehensive. You will probably manage at least a week of subsidised lunches before staff and pupils get suspicious.

Keep an eye out for summer goods that are now in the sale – for example, croquet sets are often slashed in price at this time of year. However, before you get your purse out, think, Do I really want a croquet set? If the answer is 'no', don't buy it.

Go foraging for food. Plan to spend a day a week eating food that you have found, either in the hedgerows (blackberries), on trees (apples) or just on the ground (mushrooms, but not the red ones with spots on). If this doesn't work, go to a kiddies' playground and check out the empty buggies for half-eaten rusks and Cheesy Wotsits.

If you live in the country, run over a few pheasants; they're incredibly stupid and quite easy to hit.

Even if you have been successful in your hedgerow-foraging, do not make your own chutney. For starters, you will have to buy a special pan and a thermometer (you can't use the one you bought that time you thought you had swine flu), so by the time you've paid for all the kit, you could have bought a massive catering-sized jar of Branston. Branston pickle is better than any crappy chutney you could make, especially if you are trying to use up a job-lot of rhubarb. In fact, go further than boycotting your own homemade chutney: buy shares in Branston. Since the recession, sales have gone up by 41 per cent. Forget oil – buy Branston.

Instead of faffing about making something 'homemade' simply buy any cakes or sweets and put them in a Christmas-wrapping-paper-covered box with a doily or two and you will be able to kid people you've spent hours making homemade chocolate truffles or baking.

Make your own sparklers by gluing gunpowder to kebab sticks (but not too much).

Make sure you've got a baked potato in the oven at all times: not only are they healthy, cheap and nutritious but you can pop one under the duvet and, hey presto, you've got an edible bed warmer. (NB Don't put coleslaw in the bed-warming potato.)

Remember Christmas is coming so why not decide now is the time to become a Jehovah's Witness?

Keep the festivities low-key: don't buy a Christmas tree; just put some earrings on a pot plant.

With all the money you have saved, why not bugger off somewhere hot? If you can't afford Dubai, maybe a mate has got a greenhouse you can spend a fortnight in.

Either that or check yourself into Crisis at Christmas... Leave it up to them to decide if you are a volunteer or a needy recipient.

MAKE MONEY
FROM YOUR HOUSE
(OR PIMP YOUR CRIB!)

TELLY companies are always looking for all sorts of different locations for dramas. Your house could earn good money depending on what it looks like. Nice big Victorian *Outnumbered*-style family homes, complete with very smug kitchens (Aga essential) are particularly popular and can earn about £750 a day! However, expect to earn less if your place looks like a crack den. Also remember that they don't want you hovering about trying to get your big, fat face on camera. From dawn to 3 a.m. you will have to go somewhere else, and you're not allowed to mind when hairy-arsed cameramen leave appalling stenches in your en suite.

GET a lodger. Preferably one who looks like Antonio Banderas. You don't necessarily need a spare bedroom; he can always bunk up with you. If you've got a husband, get him to kip on the sofa. These are hard times and we've all got to be prepared to make sacrifices.

HIRE your attic out to criminals who need somewhere to store stolen goods – who'd have thought that you, a respectable, Sunday-morning car-washing pillar of society would have a loft full of knock-off? No one! That's why you can charge what you like!

PRETEND that Coldplay used to rehearse in your garage. Once this rumour gets out on the Internet, loads of Coldplay fans will make pilgrimages to your address. Charge them for a peek into your garage and say stuff like, 'Yes, this is where Chris Martin thought up the name for the band. Because it was a bit draughty in the garage, he used to joke it was too "cold to play", which eventually got shortened to "Coldplay" and hence a musical legend was born.'

MAKE friends with the graffiti artist Banksy and persuade him to do a massive great mural on the side of your house – if you don't know the fella, you could always try and fake a Banksy. This, however, could land you in a mess and a bill from the council for clearing it up.

SITE-SPECIFIC theatre is very big news at the minute. Charge theatre-goers fifteen quid to see a performance artist (you) cook dinner for her family in situ. Here's a revue you can borrow: 'So true to life it could almost be real.'

IF you've got a nice big back garden, why not convert the space into dog kennels? Obviously you have to like dogs and stuff, but there's money in mutts if you don't mind the barking and the smell and the constant poop-scooping.

IF you prefer cats, then go for a cattery, or breed parrots, or those miniature pigs that everyone keeps banging on about.

IF your house is on the route to a secondary school, make a load of alternative, unhealthy packed lunches and charge the kids for them – the more junk you put in, the more they will pay. All you need do is stuff the lunchboxes with crisps, chocolate and fizzy drinks – if you bulk-buy this up front, each lunch should only cost you a quid, but because teenagers are too lazy and thick to work that out, charge them three quid.

CONVERT your basement into a dungeon and charge local masochists to come round and tie each other up down there. All you need is some black paint and manacles; the masochists will bring their own extra paraphernalia. Just don't keep popping downstairs to 'see if they're OK'. It's meant to hurt.

MAKE a Barbie 'dell' in the back garden and charge kiddies a fiver to see the 'plastic busty fairies'.

SET up a pirate radio station in your bedroom and just wait for the advertising revenue to roll in. Make even more money by offering your services as a jingle singer.

FUN THINGS TO DO
THAT DON'T COST ANY MONEY

MAKE YOURSELF AT HOME AT HOME

The trouble with having fun these days is that it can cost a heck of a lot of money, which for many of us can completely spoil the enjoyment. There's nothing like standing in a massive queue at Legoland with a load of crotchety kids demanding stupid chips to make you think, 'Well, fuck this for a game of soldiers. Bang goes my hard-earned money, wasted on a load of pathetic rides and appalling food – and still the little shits aren't the slightest bit grateful. God, I want a drink!'

So we've come up with a cost-efficient alternative to these pricey outings. Basically, unless you do something stupid, like leaving the bath running and causing thousands of pounds worth of damage by flooding the place, or accidentally setting fire to it, your home is one of the cheapest places to spend your time in. For starters, there's no service charge at mealtimes and you don't have to pay for corkage whenever you open a bottle of wine. In fact, staying at home is one of the most efficient ways of tackling the credit crunch, so make sure yours is full of fun things to do (not slot machines). Remember, it's your house, even if technically the bank owns 125 per cent of it. (Negative equity is a terrible thing.)

Given that no one can afford to go out much, you might as well make staying in as enjoyable as possible. Now, before you start thinking about getting a really massive surround-sound plasma telly, let's think of other ways that you can have fun in the comfort of your own home.

Budget Fun for the Family

In prehistoric times, before Sky+ and Wii, people had nothing to do of an evening, their entertainment consisted mostly of sucking on a bit of bread and dripping, picking one another's head lice out by candlelight and listening to *The Shipping Forecast* all the way through.

As it happens, making your own entertainment is enjoying a comeback, as teenagers have got less money than in living memory. They can't afford a new iPod or the latest computer game any more because even jobs in Greggs or Tesco where they have to wear a J Cloth on their head are in short supply. Even more tragic for them is the fact that they can't afford to go out of a night-time and are trapped indoors with their mums and dads. Ha!

PLAY FAMILY GAMES

Use your family as people to socialise and play games with. Let's face it, they're not going anywhere either, so while you're all skint and stuck at the same address, you might as well make the most of each other! Try playing cards, but not for money (or jewellery), as this can lead to family rifts. Tell your children that tiddlywinks are the new rock and roll.* Or else play boring board games at the kitchen table until the kids beg to go to bed early. Great, once they're out of the way you can get out the vodka and play strip bingo.

GET YOURSELF A TWISTER CARPET

Hey presto, permanent fun whenever you need cheering up. This might cost quite a lot to design and have made up, especially if you choose 100 per cent wool.

WHY NOT HAVE A MEASURING WALL?

Remember how you used to measure the kids when they were small? Why not measure everyone who comes round to your house? Who's the tallest, your cousin Nigel, the man who came to fix the Digi-Box or the enormous Jehovah's Witness lady? Hours of fun.†

---

* Basically, anything is the new rock and roll as long as you play it with a bottle of Jack Daniel's in your hand.
† Remember to ask permission before you measure strangers; some people can be a bit touchy about their height, particularly very short men.

INVEST IN A PIANO

The family that sings together stays together.* Back in the days before plasma televisions, on high days and holidays, when they'd had a glass of stout or some advocaat, someone would open up the front room and dust off the pianola to have what is known as 'a bit of a sing-song'. Auntie Beryl would belt out 'My Old Man Said Follow the Van' or 'Roll Out the Barrel' and everyone would sing their heads off. Eventually, an aged uncle with rickets would recite his 22-verse poem, Auntie Edna would clog-dance in her long johns, and the children would be encouraged to do their party pieces. Hours and hours would go by and everyone was truly entertained. Everyone, that is, except those between the ages of 15 and 30, who would be bored rigid. But here's the thing – they may have been bored, but at least they weren't marauding drunk in the streets half naked, throwing up in the gutter and weeing in public. And what harm did a little boredom do anyone?

HIDE AND SEEK

Make sure you (mum) get to hide. Make the seekers (those pesky kids) count to 3,000. By the time they are 'coming – ready or not', you can be at your friend Penny's house watching reruns of *Come Dine With Me*. Marvellous.

HAVE FUN WITH VEGETABLES

Not only are vegetables a cheap and reliable source of vitamins, they can also provide hours of fun.

1) First, buy your veg or, even better, dig some up from your allotment.
2) Make an attractive display.
3) Get everyone to paint their own masterpiece.
4) Cut up the potato and do some potato-printing.
5) Then make soup.

See – hours of fun and some lunch from a simple selection of root veg. Beats a silly PlayStation game anytime.

----

* Actually, this isn't always the case; in fact, it's been well documented that many singing families are wracked with alcohol and drug issues – for example the Carpenters and the Jacksons. Come to think of it, maybe the big fuck-off telly is a really good idea.

Bring Back Hobbies

Stamp-collecting, bell-ringing, draughts, dominoes and snakes and ladders are bound to once again absorb and enthral the younger generation. Women of a certain age have for some time known that they are never happier than when they are doing some colouring-in or joining the dots, with perhaps a word search for a long train journey to challenge the brain. Jigsaws will be the must-have Christmas gift, even the ones with horrible Constable paintings on them.

MAKE SURE YOU HAVE A WELL-STOCKED ART DRAWER

An art drawer might just stop you getting depressed. In this drawer you should keep glue, scissors (not too sharp), glitter, good paper, paints, felt-tips, wax crayons and pencils. There's always someone you know who would appreciate a homemade birthday card. From now on you can make all your own greetings cards, complete with little sticky-on things that fall off when you try and get them in the envelope. Or why not draw just for drawing's sake? If you make something really good, you could put it on your wall. Just don't give yourself a hard time if it's a bit crap.

HOW ABOUT SUDOKU WALLPAPER?

Someone must make it, and if they don't, just photocopy thousands of sudokus from loads of different papers and magazines and glue them to your wall – hours of fun. Particularly useful in the lavvy.

MAKE A GROTTO

Just cover your bathroom walls with copper sulphate, stand back and wait for the beautiful blue crystals to form – if it's good enough for Turner Prize nominee Roger Hiorns, it's good enough for you.*

And Not Forgetting Reading

Reading is a really good thing to do. It costs absolutely nothing, and the only equipment you need is your eyes, and maybe a pair of glasses. You can't be bored if you've got a good book. This should be law and people (mainly children) who still say they're bored should be fined.

----

* Copper sulphate is a bit toxic, so watch it.

There are loads of good books around. You can pick them up ever so cheaply from Amazon or charity shops. It's a great idea to build up a collection of good books, so that you can decide what sort of book you really like. For some reason, lots of men like reading books about battleships, whereas women like books about relationships – just make sure you choose the right book for you, otherwise there is a chance that you will hate the book and end up throwing it at the wall.

The danger of reading too many good books, however, is that you will compare yourself unfavourably to all these brilliant authors, feel stupid and uncreative, and before you know it, dark thoughts will once again be crowding your brain. The best way to temper this kind of literary low is to read some rubbish, or look at something with a lot of pictures. Men can choose from any sporting or car magazine, while women have hundreds of silly magazines with pics of food or fashion to momentarily distract them from how ghastly life is.

Forget Clubbing – It's Pricey and Tiring

How many of us have gone out on a Saturday night only to wake up on a Sunday morning with a sore head and an empty purse? Well, not any more...

Why not have your very own kitchen disco instead? All you need is a CD player, some CDs, a set of disco lights or some of those Christmas-tree lights that flash on and off (and give you a bit of a head). Get a couple of neighbours round, close the curtains and get down and boogie.

The joy of your very own kitchen disco is that as soon as you start to get a stitch, you can sit down, have a breather, maybe a nice teacake. Plus you can fit it around your plans, instead of having to go out in the cold and dark when you'd rather be watching *Casualty*. In fact, you could have an afternoon kitchen disco. Dance in your pinny if you want: there's no dress code in your club – no snotty bouncer not letting you in because you don't look like a whore. More importantly, there's a nice clean lavvy with no wee all over the toilet floor (not unless the old man's missed again).

LOLLING IS THE NEW GOING OUT

Once you have had lots of fun in your house, don't forget to relax. Of course, in the olden days, when middle-class people like you had loads of disposable income, you'd be rushing about trying to get ready in time to make it to the theatre or some concert... Well, thank goodness the recession has come along and given us all a big, fat excuse to stay in of a night-time. Hoorah – no more tedious nights at the opera, not that you ever went before, but you know what I mean.

HOW TO LOLL IN STYLE: THE RULES

✔ Make sure what you are wearing is suitable for lolling. You don't want anything that might dig in, so ideally, if you are a woman, remove your bra.

✔ Don't wear anything that you mind spilling food or drink down. If you are in full 'loll' mode, you won't be eating sitting at a table. One of the hazards of eating and lolling at the same time is food spillage and dribbling – make sure what you are wearing can easily be popped on a quick wash.

✔ Also, make sure you are wearing layers that can easily be discarded if you get hot or popped on if you feel cold.

✔ Get a load of beanbags; being comfortable is the key to staying at home. The great thing about a beanbag is that once you're in it, it's a struggle to get out. Good – as long as you've got the remote control, you won't need to move until you get hungry.

✔ Getting really hungry while you're watching TV is an occupational hazard. Make sure you are well prepared by filling the pockets of your telly-watching cardie with tubes of Pringles and sweets. Advanced lollers will also have a selection of takeaway menus to hand and a mobile phone on which to make orders. Maybe, if you have a really good relationship with a local takeaway delivery service, you can trust them with a key, so they can actually deliver your meal not just to your house, but to your lap – now that's what we call service.

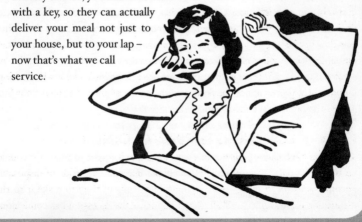

SAFETY IN THE
HOME

INSURING AGAINST **BURGLARS**

This might sound a bit basic, but it won't harm to remind you that there are people out there who will quite happily break into your house and nick all the expensive things that you have bust your gut earning money to buy over the past few years. These people must be kept out of your house, so for God's sake get some decent locks and make sure you use them. However, it's not just strangers you need to watch out for. Think – do you really trust your kids? Some teenagers have the morality of kitchen towel, so if your laptop goes missing, don't automatically jump to the conclusion that a stranger has got into your house. Maybe the finger of suspicion should point in another direction. Yes, that sixteen-year-old slob of a dope-smoking son of yours. Think about it – he's always been a shifty little twat. Are you absolutely positive that it wasn't him who flogged it so that he could buy some stupid weed?

USE YOUR HOME AS A GYM

There's no need to join an expensive gym; why not keep fit in your own home?

Lots of Stairs and a Poor Memory = Nicely Toned Legs

The best home gyms are often in those narrow Georgian houses that tend to be more staircase than anything else. What you have to do is leave something you need on the top floor and forget about it until you've made it all the way down to the basement. Now race back to the top of the house. To make this more fun, why not time yourself and see just how quickly you can do five flights of stairs? This game is more fun still if you've got a train to catch and you're wearing too many layers – gosh, look at your purple face; you really are incredibly hot and sweaty. Make sure you don't have a heart attack!

The Sitting Room as an Assault Course

Try getting round the sitting room without touching the floor. This should get you out of puff in no time at all. Invite your chums to join in. To make things trickier, swap the furniture round on a regular basis.

'Housework' Aerobics

Snooping round your teenager's bedroom trying to find evidence of drug-taking and sexual activity will work you up into a right old sweat and burn off loads of calories. Score extra points if you manage to find their diary: realising that your fifteen-year-old daughter is a bit of a slapper will put you off your food for a month.

STUPID STUFF YOU SHOULDN'T WASTE YOUR MONEY ON

Even when we're trying to count our pennies, most of us get carried away now and again and end up frittering. 'Frittering' means to spend insubstantial amounts of money on silly things. 'It's only a quid or fifty pence,' you might hear yourself say, but frittering is a bit like gambling: it's addictive, a complete waste of money and can lead to splurging, which involves spending a lot of money on silly things.

SCRATCH CARDS – no, you won't win.

SLOT MACHINES – fifteen-year-old boys are allowed to go through a phase of liking these, but if it's not all over by the time you're 20, you're in trouble. There is nothing sadder than a single adult male in an amusement arcade. Oh yes, there is: a single adult female. Now, she really *should* know better.

THOSE RIDES FOR KIDDIES IN THE SUPERMARKET – anyway, you're too old.

DRINKING IN FANCY BARS – drink at home. It's cheaper and you won't need to fork out for a cab.

MADAME TUSSAUDS – who are all those spooky people?

OVERPRICED CRÊPERIES – it's a pancake. Get over it!

SKIING HOLIDAYS – you will only get some complicated fracture of the thigh bone that will hurt for the rest of your life whenever it gets a bit cold and damp.

AN EXPENSIVE FOUNTAIN PEN – you will only lose it.

ANYTHING WRITTEN BY DAN BROWN

A MICHAEL BUBLÉ ALBUM

DUSTERS – there's no point being married if you can't use his old underpants for cleaning out the oven.

SHOES THAT DON'T FIT

ACRYLIC FINGERNAILS WITH SUNSETS AND PALM TREES PAINTED ON THEM – silly.

A PAUL SMITH TOOTHBRUSH

SELF-HELP BOOKS – do not, however, give all the ones you have already bought to charity; put every page to good use and with any luck you won't have to buy another loo roll for six months.

CATERING-SIZE JARS OF GHERKINS/TARTARE SAUCE – a) you won't be able to get the lid off; b) no one likes gherkins or tartare sauce that much; and c) it won't fit in the cupboard and you'll have to put up with the sight of it every day, sitting there on your work surface, getting in the way, until you admit defeat and chuck it in the bin.

ANYTHING YOU HAVE TO SEND OFF FOR – you like the process of browsing online or through a catalogue, but when it arrives, you'll be disappointed. For some reason, though, you won't be arsed to parcel it up and send it back – sheer, wanton waste.

ANYTHING WITH THE WORD 'EXECUTIVE' IN IT, as in *executive* room, *executive* case, *executive* seat – it's a rip-off appealing to your sense of self-importance, that tiny bit of Alan Partridge that exists in all of us. Ignore it.

Tips on Saving ENERGY in the home

As anyone who has ever played Monopoly will know, utilities cost. However, there are ways of keeping your household bills to a minimum. Here's how:

INVEST IN A LONG EXTENSION LEAD

Post it through the cat flap and over next door's fence into their garden-shed socket and, hey presto, electrical power for free!

STAY IN BED

This is the cheapest and most efficient way to keep warm. If you need an excuse, persuade yourself that you're a bit depressed – this is a great excuse to 'cheer yourself up' by eating custard creams and watching lots of daytime telly.

SHARE A BATH

But only with people you are related to or don't mind having sex with.

CUT DOWN ON HEATING BILLS

Refuse to put the central heating on till November, even if you do have to wear a sleeping bag around the house. Use up old tubes of Deep Heat and Ralgex; just rub a bit up the backs of your legs and you'll feel toasty in no time.

TURN ALL YOUR ELECTRICAL APPLIANCES OFF AT THE SOCKET BEFORE YOU GO TO BED

Obviously you will forget you have done this in the morning, panic, think you've had a power cut and call out an emergency electrician. This will cost you £90 just to be told that you have unplugged your appliances – an expensive mistake, but surely one you're not going to make twice, unless you're a complete and utter moron.

SAVE ELECTRICITY

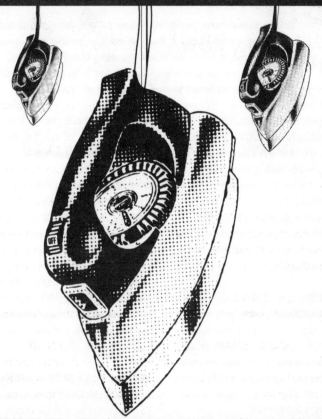

GIVE UP IRONING

WAR ON WASTE

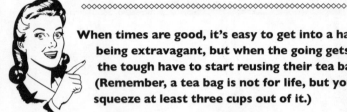

When times are good, it's easy to get into a habit of being extravagant, but when the going gets tough, the tough have to start reusing their tea bags. (Remember, a tea bag is not for life, but you can squeeze at least three cups out of it.)

MAKE THINGS LAST LONGER BY ADDING MILK OR VINEGAR This works particularly well with milk or vinegar.

CHECK THE ITEMS IN YOUR FRIDGE EVERY MORNING If something is about to go off, eat it; it's better to be fat than a waster.

DITTO CHECK YOUR FREEZER With any luck there just might be some prawns in there buried deep under a layer of ice – prawns you bought when you still had money. Defrost them right now!

BUY HIDEOUS INGREDIENTS SUCH AS TRIPE OR PIG'S LIVER Your family will only be able to stomach the teeniest portions and therefore you will save heaps of money on your weekly shopping bill.

SQUISH TOGETHER TINY SLIVERS OF SOAP TO MAKE ONE REUSABLE BAR

OPEN BIRTHDAY AND CHRISTMAS PRESENTS VERY CAREFULLY so that you can re-use the wrapping paper next year.

IF YOU WENT OUT AND GOT DRUNK LAST NIGHT check you didn't drop a kebab under the sofa at 3 a.m. – it will do for lunch.

WHEN YOU BUY A NEW PAIR OF TIGHTS make sure you keep that nice piece of stiff cardboard packaging. It's ideal for making lists, and much smarter than the back of an envelope! Just the ticket for when you're treating yourself to a shop in Waitrose rather than Lidl.

Let's Get Cooking

We all know that in these penny-pinching days we need to stop wasting our money on over-packaged, overpriced convenience foods and start making economic sense in our own kitchens – in other words, it's time we stopped being idle domestic sluts and learned how to cook. So from now on domestic-science lessons will be reintroduced into classrooms across the country, only this time round we'll start kids off when they're really little.

As soon as they enter nursery school, we will introduce them to some early-learning roll-out skills, including how to place currant eyes correctly on pastry men and, most importantly, how to pour liquids into various receptacles without being silly and making a mess.

Throughout primary school, children will be taught basic sandwich construction (thereby enabling them to make their own packed lunch), how to bake a potato and open a tin of beans without cutting themselves or spilling bean juice all over the place, the art of table-setting (including where napkins go) and how to make a nice cup of tea without incurring third-degree burns. Each of these skills will come in useful when Mummy and Daddy have got a hangover or Mummy just wants to watch *Hollyoaks* and not make supper.

Juniors will also be taught how to open a cheese triangle neatly, as too many cheese triangles are wasted due to cack-handed opening. By the time kids enter secondary school, they will be ready to learn how to peel vegetables, make stock and, crucially, clean up after themselves. At this point it might be useful to

teach them some other domestic stuff, like cleaning the bath, painting skirting boards and defrosting the freezer.

No child should be allowed to leave secondary education without being able to scramble eggs, cook a Sunday roast and rustle up three mince dishes. They should also be capable of making flapjacks without looking at a recipe, be fruit-crumble competent and proficient in the art of making soup.

Everyone needs to be kitchen-savvy. It doesn't matter how clever you are; if you aren't capable of pouring cereal into a bowl and adding milk without Coco Pops and milk going all over the lino, then you are not fit for society.

Kids would rather have plain pasta with some tomato sauce squirted into it. It's all very well trying to develop a kid's palate, but if it's just going to go to waste/end up in their hair, stick to fish fingers and frozen peas.

Home ECONOMICS

||||||||||||||||||||||||||||||||||||||||||||||||||||||||||||||||||||||||||||||||||||||||||||||||||||||||||||||||||||||

Work it out – which is cheaper, a lifetime of eating three meals a day or a gastric bypass? Hmm, decisions, decisions. Some meals are cheaper than others though. Basically, anything that is predominantly pasta is cheap, unless you are thinking of doing caviar tagliatelle. Here are some ideas for making sure you eat more cheaply.

START THE DAY THE PENNY-PINCHING WAY

Have porridge even if you don't want to – it's cheap, nutritious and has a low GI, which means you won't be reaching for the biscuit tin in 20 minutes' time, not unless you're very greedy. Real scrooges have their porridge with water and salt. That's pushing it. Have yours with skimmed milk and half a banana – make sure the other half doesn't go to waste.

Things you can do with half a banana

* Feed a small child.
* Add it to some other leftover fruit and make a lovely smoothie.
* Try it with cream cheese as a delicious lunchtime sandwich filling.
* Discard it surreptitiously on the floor of a government-owned building and accidentally slip on it. Hoorah – thousands of pounds in compensation will be yours, all yours.

REMEMBER, YOU CAN'T GO WRONG WITH A POTATO

There are 101 things you can do with a potato. Actually, there are probably more, but some of these things might be painful and/or illegal. Potatoes can be boiled, mashed, chipped, baked, croquetted and wedged. Potatoes are brilliant, but they are crap raw.

BUY A HEN!

Why? They lay eggs. Eggs are brilliant. They can be scrambled, boiled (hard, medium and soft), fried, poached, baked and omeletted. In fact, eggs might be more versatile than potatoes. They are also crap raw.

PLANT SOME VEG

If you've only got space for a window box, then stuff it with spring onions and save even more money by growing cress on a flannel. Or why don't you appropriate some local land and secretly plant some veg on it, like on a roundabout or in a small corner of your nearest park? It's easy to be surreptitious with small veg such as radishes.

SOME JOBS TO CONSIDER

Become a nurse, policeman or teacher. With any luck you'll have a subsidised canteen in your place of work. Or go for a job in the catering industry and help yourself to whatever tasty morsels come your way – maybe you could become a cake-maker? Mind you, you'd soon get sick of leftover marzipan. Even better, get a job working for a paranoid millionaire who wants all his meals tested for poison before he eats them. Of course, this could backfire if someone really does want to kill him and you end up eating poison.

HOW TO FEED A FAMILY OF FOUR WITHOUT SPENDING ANY MONEY

Simply arrive at people's houses at mealtimes; they'll be far too embarrassed not to ask you to join them. Yum, yum – tuck in.

Anything eaten with chopsticks will make you feel exotic – try spaghetti hoops.

TWENTY
FOODIE WONDERS
OF THE WORLD

Delicious meals don't need to cost a fortune; sometimes it's just a matter of eating the right thing in the right place at the right time.

- beans on toast in front of *Doc Martin*
- a small packet of iced gems after a nice swim
- a stolen lump of cheese from the fridge
- that last roast potato
- a slightly burnt sausage left over from yesterday that you unexpectedly find under the grill
- the last scraping of a homemade rice pudding
- raw cake mix
- warm bread
- crisps with wine when you're meant to be on a diet but you've drunk enough wine not to care
- Kendal mint cake eaten on top of a mountain
- cold curry
- a massive prawn
- a jam sandwich at a kiddies' party
- an entire packet of chocolate biscuits eaten in bed
- proper parkin on Bonfire Night
- a 3 a.m. kebab
- anything from M&S after you've been abroad for a fortnight
- a bacon bap with brown sauce after a bit too much red wine the night before
- a proper smelly hot dog with onions at a funfair
- wine gums on a very long car journey.

There's **NOTHING WRONG** with tap water

KITCHEN ESSENTIALS

So we've agreed we should spend more time in the kitchen. This is where the cooking action is. Before we start cooking, though...

HAVE A LOOK AT YOUR KITCHEN

Do you like it? If the answer is 'no', then no wonder you don't spend any time in it – maybe you should get a new kitchen. Unfortunately, these cost anything from a couple of grand to around a million, depending whether you opt for Ikea self-assembly or something involving an aquarium, revolving teriyaki plate and a solid-gold fridge.

Hmm... Can't afford a new kitchen? Then let's think about making the kitchen you've got more user-friendly. For starters, clean it: it's no good embarking on a cooking spree if it's going to give you botulism. You don't need a new kitchen; you just need a big bottle of bleach and some elbow grease.

OK, now that your kitchen is no longer insanitary, let's kit it out with some essentials that will save you money in the long run.

WHAT YOU NEED

A kettle
For hot drinks and the occasional emergency Pot Noodle.

A toaster
For making toast and keeping your hands warm – think of it as a little radiator.

A tea cosy
This will keep a big pot of tea warm for a really long time, which means you don't end up throwing away a big pot of tea just because it's cold. Money saved in a year: £2.

OTHER USES FOR TEA COSIES

• Say, for example, you need to go out in your dressing gown to chip ice off your car windscreen before you go to work – just pop a tea cosy on your head and it will keep you toasty. Wear rubber gloves for this job – woollen gloves just get really wet, and you don't want to spoil your good leather gloves.

• Putting a tea cosy sideways on your head will automatically turn you into an admiral, like Nelson. This could be very useful should you need to go to a fancy-dress party.

• Hiding sex toys in – who would ever guess?

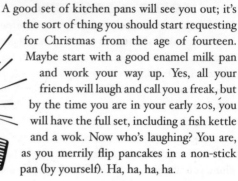

Pans

A good set of kitchen pans will see you out; it's the sort of thing you should start requesting for Christmas from the age of fourteen. Maybe start with a good enamel milk pan and work your way up. Yes, all your friends will laugh and call you a freak, but by the time you are in your early 20s, you will have the full set, including a fish kettle and a wok. Now who's laughing? You are, as you merrily flip pancakes in a non-stick pan (by yourself). Ha, ha, ha, ha.

Spoons

Get a few wooden ones. These are necessary for stirring all those tasty soups and casseroles you're going to be cooking. They're also good for the corrective training of men, children and pets.

Knives

Three will do: a bread knife, a carving knife and a small, really sharp knife that could come in handy for all sorts of things (maybe hide this knife in a special place).

Barbecue tongs

Not just for barbecues; basically incredibly useful for turning meat over. Can also be used to pinch people.

A veg peeler

A good investment – saves time and can't accidentally open a main artery.

A blender

So useful for blending soup, cake mix and paint.

WHY EVERYONE SHOULD OWN A PAIR OF RUBBER GLOVES

Rubber gloves can be used for removing things you don't want to touch from places you really don't want to put your hands (such as toilets, cows' arses and the salad tray after you've been away for three weeks); as a cheap rubber fetish accessory; pretending to be a doctor.

An apron

One of those wipe-down ones might be a good idea, as the novice cook will often be covered in blood, sweat and tears. It's so much more practical if all these secretions can simply be wiped off with a damp sponge.*There is nothing sillier than attempting to cook something in order to save money only to completely blow your good intentions by getting massive greasy gravy splodges on your new cream cashmere cardie. Wear a pinny, you silly girl, and if you wear glasses, remember they will steam up when you open the oven door. Don't panic – this is a temporary thing; you haven't suddenly gone blind!

----

* Buy some sponges for wiping down all sorts of surfaces. Remember to throw them away when they get smelly.

WHAT YOU DON'T NEED

* anything you don't have space for
* a plasma telly
* an electronic pepper mill – really, it's not that hard
* a deep-fat fryer – more dangerous than keeping a loaded gun in the house.

Other silly gadgets

One of the most dangerous and potentially bankrupting things a woman (particularly one who isn't getting enough sex) can do is browse through the Lakeland catalogue. There are things

in there that you never dreamed anyone could possibly need, but suddenly you'll start thinking, 'Well, if some other bitch has got a perfect-tear kitchen-roll dispenser, then why shouldn't I?'

Stay away from the Lakeland catalogue. One look and you will be hooked – before you know it, you'll be on their website at 3 a.m. scoring magnetic knife racks and ceramic Santa cruet sets.

THAT SAID, YOU DO NEED SOME TUPPERWARE

Tupperware is like a good mattress: it's a sound investment. Why do you need Tupperware? So that you can have a packed lunch, you idiot.

Obviously some people don't require a packed lunch – for example people who work from home. These people don't need a packed lunch because they are their own bosses and can have a pick at whatever they fancy from the fridge whenever they want, which is why so many of them have a weight problem.

Cheap imitations will only leak and be more trouble than they're worth; Tupperware will last until you leave it in the kitchen at work and someone nicks it. However, Tupperware isn't just for packed lunches; it also comes in handy if you fancy a picnic.

THE DIFFERENCE BETWEEN A PACKED LUNCH AND A PICNIC

A packed lunch is usually eaten at a place of work or somewhere within walking distance of work – maybe on a park bench. When you're having a packed lunch in the office, it's not usual to get out a tartan rug and sit on it while you eat; neither is it normal to set up a game of rounders, not unless you've got a really big office.

Having a packed lunch is a great way of saving money – trouble is, lots of people get into a packed-lunch rut and end up eating the same thing day after day. To make sure this doesn't happen, why not make your lunch wearing a blindfold? That way, whatever you've put in your sandwich will be a surprise. Or maybe ask a stranger to swap lunches with you on the train – who knows, you might make a new friend and get into a friendly competitive gourmet packed-lunch trumping game. Alternatively, you'll never see that good piece of lock-down Tupperware again.

SHE WHO COOKS

MUST NOT

STACK THE DISHWASHER

Stocking Your Store Cupboard

You will need:

* AS MANY HERBS AND SPICES as you can afford/know what to do with
* SOME FANCY VINEGAR and some cheap stuff for chips
* DITTO OIL – although avoid 'extra virgin' oil, nothing can be 'extra virgin', you're either a virgin or not
* FLOUR – plain and self-raising
* SUGAR – icing, brown and normal
* SALT AND PEPPER – black, not white, because no one uses white pepper any more unless they're over 65 and live in the North
* OATS – the great thing about oats is that they make you randy but are cheaper than Viagra. (Warning: might only work on horses)
* HONEY – there is nothing like honey on toast to make you feel like you are six years old again and that all you need to do is lie on your tummy reading comics and the world will be all right
* TINNED GOODS (especially beans and pulses – much easier than the dried variety, which have to be soaked for 24 hours before you know you might want to eat them)
* TINS OF TOMATOES AND COCONUT MILK – this will give anyone who snoops through your kitchen cupboard the impression that you know how to cook. Warning: they will expect you to be able to knock up a Thai green chicken curry. (No, the chicken is not meant to be green)
* CANDLES – not to eat, but in case there is a power cut or you want your food to look more appetising
* SOME CRISPS to eat while you are waiting for your healthy, nutritious and inexpensive home-cooked grub to actually cook.

And Don't Forget Stock Cubes

What if you've forgotten to buy stock cubes? For an alternative meaty stock, why not use bathwater? Or, for a nice, beefy-smelling bath, why not crumble an Oxo cube under the tap? Hmm, lie back, relax and smell the gravy.

LET'S NOT
FORGET LEFTOVERS

Apparently, it's a well-known fact that everyone in the country wastes a million pounds a year each by throwing away uneaten food. This has got to stop. From now on leftovers are on the menu. So here are some ideas about what to do with things you didn't manage to finish:

- **Leftover mash** – add some other bits and bobs to make bubble and squeak, or pipe it along the windowsill to stop that draught.
- **Leftover sausage** – don't be silly; this never happens, not unless one accidentally rolls away into a far corner of the grill pan.
- **Leftover cooked liver** – full of iron. Cut it up into small squares and give it to the family at breakfast time instead of pricey iron tablets.
- **Leftover rice** – whatever you do with leftover rice, make sure you reheat it properly: badly reheated rice causes more tummy complaints than anything else, which is ideal if you want a couple of days off work.
- **Leftover pasta** – add water and boil until it turns into glue, then store carefully. One day you might be able to use this to hang wallpaper.
- **Leftover slice of ham** – either put it in a sandwich or laminate it and, hey presto, an amusing bookmark!
- **Leftover tuna salad** – lunch or fancy cat food! Basically, if the cat turns its nose up, then it's your duty to finish it off.
- **Leftover Victoria sponge** – soak it in sherry, break it up and use it as the base for a really lovely trifle, or simply pour yourself a glass of sherry and dip in the stale cake. Makes a change from coffee at elevenses.
- **Leftover raw pastry** – add food colouring and bingo! – brightly coloured modelling clay. Why not make something, cook it and eat it?
- **Remember, most leftovers** can be turned into soup.*

----

* But not lemon meringue pie.

HOW TO SAVE MONEY IN RESTAURANTS

In restaurants, fill up with bread (even more effective if you're wheat intolerant, as by the time you've ordered you'll be so uncomfortably bloated that you won't be able to manage pudding or even the cheese board). Money saved: £8, maybe.

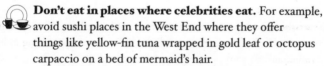

Don't eat in places where celebrities eat. For example, avoid sushi places in the West End where they offer things like yellow-fin tuna wrapped in gold leaf or octopus carpaccio on a bed of mermaid's hair.

If you accidentally end up in a really posh restaurant that is going to cost you a fortune, pretend to have toothache and ask for the soup.

Keep your coat with you, rather than put it in the cloakroom. This will save you from having to give the cloakroom attendant a tip. Money saved: £1.

Ask for a doggy bag. But make sure your leftovers can get you out of making your child a packed lunch in the morning. Think. There's nothing wrong with sending the kids to school with leftover monkfish risotto in their packed lunch but will your nine-year-old really want a congealed lump of lobster thermidor in his lunchbox?

BEING THE HOSTESS WITH THE MOSTEST

(WHILE SPENDING THE LEASTEST), OR

HOW TO HAVE A DINNER PARTY ON THE CHEAP

....

Some say the dinner party is under threat of extinction. Who says this? I do. I've stopped bothering – it's too much of a faff. However, you've got to have your mates round now and again (just to prove you've still got some), and if middle-aged folk are going to prised away from their tellies of an evening, then you have to tempt them with something, and that something is usually food and booze. The formal dinner party might have had its day – not many people seem to be bothering with origami napkins, long Laura Ashley dresses and place names – but the kitchen supper party is very much in vogue. Let's face it, not many of us can afford to eat in fancy restaurants these days, so the next best thing is to stuff your face at a mate's house. The thing is, although we all know there's a recession going on, none of us really expects beans and baked potatoes when we are invited out for dinner; however, none of us wants to spend our shoe fund on feeding our friends. What a dilemma!

The solution, of course, is to make out that a great deal of time, money and effort has gone into your feast while actually forking out very little, and the trick to having a supper party that looks more expensive than it actually is is to cheat.

HINTS FOR CHEATING

If you are giving a dinner party and have nothing to wear, pop a stripy butcher's apron over whatever you're wearing and at least you'll look professional. Professional cook's pinnies are great; not only do they cover bulgy bits and greasy old stained clothing, but they will also lull the guests into thinking that you are an expert cook. Now that you have lulled them into this false sense of security, you can serve any old cheap rubbish, and as long as you present the meal as if it's been extremely complicated to cook and the ingredients cost a fortune, then they will fall for it. This tip only really works if you are hosting the dinner party; if you're a guest, it might look rather strange.

For that 'I've been slaving away over a hot stove all day' look, remember not to put on any deodorant or make-

up. Just one whiff of your sweaty pits and the sight of your blotchy red face will remind everyone that you've been flogging your guts out for them, the selfish parasites.

Make sure you leave lots of professional-looking pans out on the work surface; those ornamental copper ones you normally hang on the wall will do. The filthier they are, the better. In fact, litter your entire kitchen with every single utensil that you have been given for Christmas and birthdays. This will encourage your pals to think that you've actually bothered to make your own bread and ice cream. After all, why else would you have the equipment to do so out? Chuck some jam and coffee over your River Café cookbook; this will give the impression that you actually use the thing.

Remember, everything sounds posher in a foreign language. Try serving *saucisses et purée* or *une baguette du beurre de cacahuètes*. Or else buy really scraggy bits of red meat and pretend it's reindeer or smoked puffin breast.

Serve thin slices of ancient loofah and pretend it's putrefied Greenland shark – a delicacy so disgusting that it couldn't taste any worse than ancient loofah. (It is actually possible to harvest your own loofah. This is entirely true – look it up on the Internet. Honestly, I am not mad. You can buy loofah seeds and grow your own crop of the bath-time accoutrement. True.)

Insist that corned-beef hash is the new sushi. Actually, anything can be the new sushi as long as it's small and brightly coloured – for example, as a cheap and exotic pudding, why not serve Liquorice Allsorts on a big platter and introduce them as the new 'sweet sushi'?

WATCH THE EXPERTS

All you need to do to make cheap food look expensive is watch *MasterChef* and pick up some tips about fashionable dishes and how to serve them. At the moment there is a lot of plate-smearing going on; the fashionable dinner plate these days looks like something that needs to go in the dishwasher. Basically, all you need is a square of meat or fish with a purée of something brightly coloured smeared around it. Frozen peas whizzed in the blender with some yoghurt and mint will do. Use swede but say it's kohlrabi.

Remember, everything is edible and smart if it has a balsamic reduction zigzagged over it. The zigzagging is important, and if you can buy some really big white plates, maybe from a seconds shop, they will make everything look more restauranty. In fact, making the dinner party properly restauranty is a jolly good idea, so why not design your own menu? And maybe get an aged relative to pretend to be a lavatory attendant. All they need do is sit in your bathroom with a saucer containing loose change and hand paper towels to your customers – I mean friends.

If you are going to play restaurants, you will have to offer a choice. Once your guests have made their selections, you can tell them that actually the *moules* are off and Chef has run out of game terrine; however, there is some very nice tomato soup available. No one will know your soup is tinned as long as you put sherry in it. The ratio is two parts tinned tomato soup to one part sherry.*

At the end of the meal, you can

---

* It's not just tomato soup that benefits from having a load of booze chucked in; anything that is cheap and shop-bought will automatically taste different once you've added alcohol. However, lager is tricky to make work. Add lager to anything and it automatically tastes like something a tramp would have for breakfast. Have a really good look at the back of your cupboards; there's bound to be something truly vile lurking in there. Calvados and custard, for example, is a real winner. Brandy is excellent because it's also flammable, so whatever you cook, if it looks a bit boring, just slosh it with brandy, set it on fire and bring it to the table while it's still burning.

give your guests their bill. This looks best on a small silver dish containing a couple of mints. If you can't find any Polos knocking about, check the kids' schoolbags – they'll probably have a couple of sticks of gum gathering fluff at the bottom. Most of your guests will be too drunk and shocked not to stump up. If any of them do protest, you can always lose that expensive coat of theirs in the cloakroom and keep it ransom until they cough up.

The great thing about restaurants is that in the morning your guests won't believe it really happened; they will think they imagined it and possibly make a doctor's appointment to talk about how many units really are safe.

ADVANCED STINGINESS: HOW TO GET OUT OF SPENDING ANY MONEY ON FOOD AND WINE

Invite some friends over for dinner but make sure the arrangements are rather complicated, with lots of phone calls discussing lots of potential dates. Eventually, after changing your mind several times, opt for 'a week on Friday'. When a week on Friday comes, make sure you are sat in front of the telly when they turn up. Then show them your diary, which will clearly state that dinner is next Friday! The chumps!

Oh well, now they're here, you can always have an impromptu dinner party. Of course it's not too much trouble. Shame you haven't been to the supermarket and all that, but you've got some fig rolls and a bottle of brandy. Hey presto, dinner for four for under a tenner.

Obviously now it's going to be their turn to host supper. Only this time, make sure you have diaries out and that there can't possibly be any misunderstanding.

DEGREE-LEVEL STINGINESS

Get a load of friends round and make a big hoo-ha about ordering from a really expensive Chinese takeaway. Insist on paying for everyone and make sure they hear you order and give your credit-card details over the phone. Two hours later when the Chinese hasn't turned up (because you never actually called), phone them up, have a huge row and tell your guests the Chinese lost your order and now the kitchen is closing. Squeeze some tears out – everyone will feel really sorry for you. After all, you were prepared to spend a fortune. What a shame it hasn't worked out. Oh well, you've got some peanut butter and you can always get some bread out of the freezer. What a great gal you are!

CHEAP CHIC

Unless you have a job that involves a uniform – for example, fireman, policeman or McDonald's employee – we all have to think about getting dressed in the morning. For some people, this is simply a question of picking up what's on the bedroom floor, sniffing the armpits/crotch and, if it doesn't stink, putting it on. For others, getting dressed means spending hours in front of the mirror trying to decide whether something makes you look weird, fat or desperate.

Fact

Ninety-eight per cent of the female workforce has at some point taken a day off work pretending to be sick when in reality the only reason they can't go to work is because they can't decide what to wear. This is when a pair of black trousers comes in handy. Unless you want to be mistaken for a waitress, however, do not team these with a white shirt.

Decisions, Decisions

Another dilemma for many people at the moment is deciding which is cheaper, continuing to smoke and staying exactly the same size or giving up smoking and having to buy an entire new wardrobe in six months' time because you've managed to put on three stone. Well, the answer to this (based on a 20-a-day smoker) is that if you give up the evil weed, you will save yourself two grand a year, which will buy you lots of nice floral tent-like dresses from Evans. Result!

No Rules
Are the New Rules

One of the great things about being in a recession is that we no longer have to be slaves to fashion; in fact, wearing designer labels is rather vulgar at the moment and to be honest shrieks 'Russian hooker'. These days it's de rigueur to mix and match. The well-dressed woman will be wearing a little bit of vintage with a soupçon of high street, plus something she found in a skip. This is fashion. The great thing about not having to stick to any rules is that no one is allowed to say that what you're wearing is wrong – unless you're me, in which case it probably is. However, many people get very confused about not having any cohesive rules to follow, which is why some women panic and buy complete outfits from Per Una.

Clothes-share

Why not share a wardrobe with a fellow yo-yo dieter? Chances are, you won't both be 'thin' at the same time and can therefore share those skinny jeans and body-con frocks as well as the kaftans and jumbo jogging bottoms.

!!!WARNING!!!
THE DANGERS OF PER UNA

Developing a Marks & Spencer Per Una habit is something one must avoid at all costs. Per Una is the heroin of middle-aged ladies' clothing: you start with just a little bit of Per Una – maybe a cardigan in jade with some beading round the neckline – and the next thing you know, your wardrobe is bulging with appliquéd skirts and embroidered jumpers. You go out and you're Per Una-ed from head to foot; you look like a great big enormous tea cosy. Stay away from the Per Una.

THE TRUTH ABOUT WOMEN AND CLOTHES

❀

All a woman really wants is to be thin enough to wear a pair of jeans and white T-shirt. It is possible to feel a million dollars for under £60.

What Is the Difference Between Vintage and Second-Hand?

As you will have read in magazines, lots of people in the fashion know are wearing vintage, but how can you tell what is genuinely vintage?

- -

Vintage is something Kate Moss would wear. Second-hand is that thing you picked up from the Sue Ryder shop.

- -

Also, vintage is not a hand-me-down, unless your nana was Coco Chanel. For example, if you ask Kate Moss what she is wearing, she might reply, 'An original Yves Saint Laurent.' She will probably not say, 'Oh, this? It used to belong to Agyness Deyn.'

Hand-Me-Downs

These include things like:

- ☺ a pair of pyjamas that have been so wee-soaked over the years that the crotch has rotted out
- ☺ a cardigan that went on a hot wash and has turned into felt
- ☺ a school shirt that has got an older relative's name sewn into the collar
- ☺ something with frayed cuffs because the person who wore it first was a cuff-chewer
- ☺ a velvet party dress with a Ribena-stained collar.

In the old days, people often felt self-conscious and a bit poor wearing hand-me-downs, but now that everyone's gone green, wearing clothes that have been recycled is very cool indeed. In fact, the more like a tramp you look, the better. Just don't start drinking cider on park benches in the morning.

- -

Remember:
There's nothing wrong with hand-me-downs.
Wear your hand-me-downs with pride.

- -

When I was a child, hand-me-downs were an occupational hazard, as I was the second daughter of tight-fisted Northern parents. (Note: it's much crueller for parents to inflict an older sister's clothes on a younger brother. In fact, if your mum and dad try this, you could probably sue them for child cruelty. The kilt, of course, will always be a grey area.) My worst ever hand-me-down experience dates back to 1973 and involved a tweed trouser suit that once belonged to my cousin Elizabeth, an abomination of an outfit that made me itch so much that I scratched until I bled. My mother thought I was just showing off.

Most of my hand-me-downs were donated to me by my older sister. I got so fed up with these limp and worn rags that I decided to put on enough weight for it to be physically impossible for me to squeeze into her cast-offs. By systematically eating all the wrong things for a period of time, I soon weighed two stone more than her. Ha, ha, I won.

Actually, I didn't. My mother simply dressed me in hand-me-downs from my morbidly obese grandmother. Great.

Out of sheer spite I then went on a silly diet and developed the potentially life-threatening eating disorder anorexia nervosa – thus by the time I was in my early 20s I was wearing hand-me-downs from seven-year-olds.

MAKE YOUR OWN CLOTHES

SEWING

All you need is a sewing machine. A good one will cost you about £300 and will weigh a ton, so try not to drop it on your foot. Then you need to buy cotton and stuff and some fabric and a pattern. Then you will have to phone your mum and have a cry. Do not open that bottle of wine.

What happens with sewing machines is that only 0.1 per cent of the population have a sewing-machine mentality. These are the people who can cheerfully make their own curtains. The rest of the population will put the sewing machine on the kitchen table and get jam on the needle, which will render it un-threadable because it's all jammy – at this point, most sensible people will put the sewing machine in a cupboard next to the breadmaker and foot spa, and forget all about it.

KNITTING

Knitting is easier than sewing, unless you're left-handed, in which case both will defeat you. First, buy a cardie from a charity shop, unravel it and then set about knitting a similar-looking cardie in the same colour! Well done.

CUSTOMISING

Tie-dyeing is one way of jazzing up a plain white T-shirt. If you can't be bothered with all that messing about with dye and rubber gloves, then another way of customising a plain white T-shirt is to simply cut out two nipple holes in the chest area – hey presto, a lovely fetish T-shirt all ready to wear to a bondage party (should you ever get invited to one).

SILLY VERSUS Sensible

Here are some examples of Silly Fashion: White jeans, especially white jeans on Liz Hurley (almost too silly to bear); peep-toe boots – yes, these have been in the shops (very silly); short-sleeved coats (just silly); anything that has to be dry-cleaned (silly!). Instead, why not wear sensible clothes that are made to last?

The beauty of tweed

Tweed is the least silly fabric known to man. Tweed means no-nonsense. A woman in a tweed skirt is not afraid to show you the back of her hand or use a ruler if necessary or even a big stick. The great thing about tweed is that it's almost impossible to wear out. Once you've got a tweed skirt, you've got a skirt for life. Plus it goes with everything: dog hairs, gravy stains, even a bit of amniotic fluid from a foal being born.

Why everyone should have an Aran jumper

Aran jumpers are a bit like tweed skirts: they will see you out. An Aran jumper is more or less indestructible. Even the most voracious of moth can't cope with chewing its way through the sinewy Aran fibres.

Why buy brogues?

Brogues are a good walking shoe. A brogue will carry you far and wide, through damp and boggy terrain. (Obviously not too boggy – you'd need wellies for proper bog-walking.) A sturdy brogue might be pricey to buy, but it's the shoe that makes the most economic sense. It also goes well with Aran and tweed. Bob's your uncle, a pair of brogues (lace-up and brown, preferably) to team with your tweed skirt* and Aran jumper is just the finishing touch that you need for that sensible-woman-about-town look. This is a uniform that screams, 'Don't rip me off, don't try to mug me, and don't even dream of dropping that sweetie wrapper in my vicinity.'

----

* Men can opt for a pair of corduroy trousers rather than the tweed skirt.

Some sensible accessories

* **AN UMBRELLA** – for prodding people who aren't taking any notice of you
* **A WICKER BASKET** – for wet fish from the fishmonger's or meat from the butcher's
* **A COMPASS** – this can be hung round your neck like a pendant. Hey presto, fashionable and useful.

What to do in summer

Unfortunately, your Aran, tweed and brogue combo is not going to be suitable all year round; there will be a few days in the summer when the Aran just isn't going to cut the mustard and the tweed skirt will make sweat drip down the backs of your legs and into your brogues. Getting all hot and bothered is not a good look, not when we are trying to soldier on in a calm and dignified fashion. Therefore we need a simple summer uniform.

A gay dirndl

Is just the ticket for those warm summer days. Team your dirndl with a fresh blouse (100 per cent cotton) and a simple pair of sandals. Think Julie Andrews – capable but firm, and good with children. Make sure you have a tartan rug and a picnic hamper at the ready.

Sensible clothes – a final thought

Considering so many women get depressed about their size, it's time we changed our attitude to labelling. Wouldn't it be more sensible to have:

* an **8** is a 'silly'
* a **10** is a 'smug'
* a **12** is a 'well done'
* a **14** is a 'nice'
* a **16** is an 'average'
* an **18** is a 'curvy'
* a size **20** is a 'cuddly'.
* Anything **larger** than a size 20 can be labelled 'large cuddly', 'extra-large cuddly' and 'dangerously extra-large cuddly'.

The Chin Up Guide to
Beauty

Even though it's shallow and silly, most of us are obsessed with our looks. More specifically, most of us are obsessed with looking younger than we actually are. This is possibly because youth is beautiful and old age is a bit ugly. Now, this might not be fair, but it's true: you never hear a bloke at a bar saying, 'Phwoar, she was gorgeous! About sixty but looked at least seventy. Long grey hair, covered in wrinkles and with tits right down to her knees.' Thus women are terrified of the ageing process and will do what they can to fight it. But how?

Of course, as we all know, beauty is only skin deep, but how deep is that? Who knows? Probably ███████,* who has had so many facial peels that she's about one layer of epidermis away from the bone. (Note to ███████: stop the facial peels now. Any more and you're going to look like something hanging up in a butcher's window.) The trouble with plastic surgery is that it can go wrong and patients can end up looking like they fell out of a plate-glass window while fighting with an elephant and other people just look like they've been chewed during the night by a giant moth. So here at Chin Up Britain we have devised some cunning ways of looking younger without resorting to the knife.

*Whose name did I want to put here?

THE FOUR COMMANDMENTS OF ENDLESS YOUTH

(1) **Get rid of your mirrors**. The thing is, most of us feel good when we're looking good, so if you're fed up with feeling like shit because you look like shit, then why not get rid of all the mirrors in your house? There, that's better isn't it, now that you don't have to catch sight of that hideous old boiler any more? As long as you aren't faced with the physical evidence of your hideous decay on a daily basis, you can con yourself into thinking that actually you're a bit of a hot tamale – eventually, with any luck you will develop the opposite of body dysmorphia and go around behaving like a sex siren while looking like a bag lady. Well done, scary lady.

(2) **Beauty is in the eye of the beholder,** so make sure the beholder is short-sighted.

(3) **Remember, as you get older,** the one thing you've got left on your side is perspective. The further away you are, the better you will look. (Most of us look great to a pissed bloke with cataracts who is standing half a mile away, especially if it happens to be foggy.)

(4) **Do nothing.** If you want to look good for life without resorting to plastic surgery, then all you need do is nothing; seriously – an immobile face stays younger longer. Laughing is disastrous for the complexion as it causes crow's feet, and crying is just as bad, so whatever you do, don't watch anything that will make you laugh and/or cry, which rules out *The Jeremy Kyle Show*.

⋯ Fact ⋯

People with no personality and very little sense of humour tend to look quite good for their age, in much the same way as your average chain hotel. Heavy-drinking types with a history of smoking and late nights look fantastic – like an ancient, crumbling palazzo.

Beauty on a Budget

Of course, it's not just cosmetic surgery that's a bit pricey; it's all those other little bits and bobs that the beauty industry cons us into buying that can end up costing a fortune. Well, not any more – for those of you who want to look chic on the cheap, here are some indispensable ideas:

- **Dry your towels on the line,** rather than in an expensive tumble-dryer. They will dry all horrible and stiff. Good. This means when you use them on your body, you'll get a free exfoliation. Careful not to draw blood!
- **Get a really ugly best friend.** She won't cost you anything, but standing next to her will make you look a million dollars.
- **Save money on nail varnish** by cutting your nails quite short before applying the polish. Over the next decade this will save you, on average, a pot of nail varnish. Remember, look after the pennies and the pounds will look after themselves (eventually).
- **Also, save on foundation** by not applying it to the skin on your face that is hidden by your fringe. If you don't have a fringe, just cut one. This might make you look idiotic, but it's worth the risk.
- **Do good works** and therefore be too busy and smug to bother with your looks. Secretly people will still think you look a mess but will feel like complete cows for saying so out loud.
- **Save money on buying expensive cosmetics** by stealing from your friends' make-up bags. This is less risky than nicking stuff from department stores. If they catch you at it, just say you were 'borrowing' it and laugh in a guilt-free manner. (Note: practise laughing in a guilt-free manner; the ability to pull off the guilt-free laugh is likely to get you out of all kinds of scrapes.)

LARD

KNITTED BREAST ENHANCERS

ANOTHER CHIN UP BUDGET BUSTER!

WORRIED ABOUT YOUR BUST SIZE? DON'T RESORT TO EXPENSIVE PLASTIC SURGERY.
WHY NOT KNIT YOUR OWN BREAST ENHANCERS?
HEY PRESTO, A LOVELY, BIG, COST-EFFECTIVE BOSOM MADE OF ENTIRELY WASHABLE NATURAL FIBRES.

DIY *Pamper Day*

Another outrageous expense suffered more or less entirely by the female half of the population is the spa experience. Every day thousands of women are stripped of their clothes and their dignity, and while they're feeling vulnerable in a white towelling dressing gown, they're manipulated into all kinds of expensive treatments involving seaweed and mud. Wake up, women! These places are taking the piss – you don't need to spend a fortune in the spa... Why not treat yourself to a DIY pamper day?

HARD SKIN

For starters, you don't need a fancy pedicure; just put some newspaper down on the bathroom floor and remove the hard yellow skin from your feet yourself with a cheese grater. However, do remember that these dry-heel shavings are not cheese and should never be used instead of Parmesan.

WRINKLES

Getting rid of wrinkles professionally is really expensive, so why not fashion your own Botox out of weedkiller and get a pal you trust to inject it into your face? Or why not invest in one of those fat, wrinkly Shar Pei dogs? By comparison you'll feel as smooth as a baby's bottom (or Louis Walsh's face).

CELLULITE

For stubborn cellulite (and is there any other type?), get a pal to beat the orange peel out of the back of your legs with a meat tenderiser and promise to do exactly the same for her.

ELECTROLYSIS

If you have a slightly stubbly upper lip, the sort of thing that looks a bit like a hairy caterpillar wriggling around under your nose, apply gaffer tape to the offending area, press on really hard and then simply strip away the gaffer complete with moustache. Also works in the pants area.

Many women get very uptight about their bikini area. Personally, I don't know why they call it the 'bikini area' when some of my pubic hairs are growing down behind my knees. I actually think that we should bring back the bush – the Brazilian's had its day; it's time to reclaim the pube. So sport your stragglers with pride. Let it all hang out at the local swimming pool, and encourage pubic growth with Fisons. You know it makes sense. What we want is pubes that grow halfway up our backs and down to our ankles. Yes, save on fuel bills this winter: keep warm thanks to a big, furry pubic pelt.

If we all put one of these stickers on our car,
we just might save the pubic bush.

Clothes Shopping

FOR MOST WOMEN, SHOPPING IS IN THE BLOOD. We can't help it – it's a medical fact that women who are prevented from shopping can go mad. This is why it's important in these troubled economic times to continue to shop but to shop steadily and sensibly. Keeping your shopping on an even keel will prevent outbreaks of binge-shopping.

At the top of the shopping scale is, of course, clothes shopping – we're not talking about buying the kids their school uniforms or the old man's vests here; we're talking proper clothes.

DESIGNER CLOTHES

Don't be silly – you may look in the window; you may dribble on the window, but then walk away. These threads are not for the likes of you. Anyway, you wouldn't get the trousers further than your knees, fatty.

NORMAL CLOTHES SHOPPING – THE RULES

(1) **Always try it on.**
(2) **Don't be afraid to ask** a stranger for their opinion. They have nothing to lose by telling you that you look 'fucking appalling', which is exactly what happened to me in Whistles recently.
(3) **If you need help getting it on or off,** it's too small.
(4) **Don't buy anything** that doesn't match anything that you've already got.
(5) **Don't buy it** if you only like the colour 'in a certain light'.
(6) **Don't buy it** if it's very similar indeed to something you've already got.
(7) **If you do buy it** and you're not sure, put the receipt safely in your purse.
(8) **Keep the bag.** You've got more chance of getting your money back if the item of clothing is returned in the bag it came in, complete with hanger – even if you've worn it out five times, got lipstick on it, and the truth is, you just got a bit bored with it.
(9) **If they offer you** a free coat-hanger when you buy something in a shop, take it.

FOOD SHOPPING

Further down the shopping scale is food shopping. All of us need to go shopping for food now and again – even men (ha, ha – joke). However, we should all learn to shop more efficiently. Remember, *careless* shopping costs a lot more than *careful* shopping.

MARKETS – ARE THEY WORTH IT?

Of course, ideally we should be sourcing our fruit and veg from a local street market, but the trouble with local street markets is that unless you live near London's Borough Market, the pickings are likely to be a bit slim.

In recent years street markets have divided into two camps: the smug organic farmers' Saturday-morning 'Aren't we marvellous? Here, have a taste of this dried otter' type, and the ones where you can buy knock-off phone batteries, net curtains and Barbie flick knives. If you want to save money, go to the latter. Just don't buy your fruit and veg there, because a bloke with gold teeth and a metal plate in his head who calls you 'treacle' will show you a load of juicy oranges and as soon as you agree to buy some will palm you off (in front of your very eyes) with a load of wizened, sour Sevilles and you won't even realise till you've got home!

Do yourself a favour: go to the supermarket instead.

SUPERMARKET SHOPPING

The thing about supermarkets is that they range in value and price. Unless you're feeling flush, don't go to expensive supermarkets – keep to the cheap end of the high street. It will be a depressing experience with very little to tempt you – a bit like living in Russia back in the 1960s. The trouble with expensive supermarkets is that once you step inside, your taste buds will start to tingle and you'll crave things you never even knew you wanted. Before you know it, you will have spent 36 quid on reindeer pâté. Stick to the cheaper supermarkets and make sure you buy their own-brand goods – try not to let this get you down.

OTHER WAYS TO SAVE MONEY IN THE SUPERMARKET

Before you go shopping, think, Do I really need anything? If the answer is 'yes', then make a list, and whatever you do, remember to take your list with you. Don't forget your bag for life; some food outlets have started charging for their carriers.

 Stick to the list. If that green Tu cardie, the *Cranford* DVD and a bottle of Reggae Reggae Sauce aren't on it, leave them – do not make impulse purchases, and whatever you do, if you're going out for a tin of tomato soup, don't come home with one of those little Fiat 500s. (Ah, they're so sweet, though – like the automobile equivalent of a likkle puppy.)

 Never go to the supermarket when you're hungry, hormonal or have just been dumped.

 Remember, some food costs more than other food. For example, there is a difference between wagyu steak and bog-standard mince. Wagyu cattle live in feng shui stables, are hand-massaged by virgin geishas and fed on sake and beer. Normal cattle spend their lives living knee-deep in their own shit and eating a diet of mouldy cereal, hence the difference in price. Basically, most wagyu cattle live better than you do. There is a reason why Lidl don't do tinned caviar and there's no such thing as own-brand foie gras (and if there was, you really wouldn't want to eat it. God knows what it would have in it).

HINT

Get friendly with a lady who works in your local supermarket. With any luck she will text you whenever they've got a taste-test going on or a particularly good two-for-one offer.

The thing is, millions of pounds have been spent in order to lure us around the supermarket and trick us into buying bright, shiny things that we don't really need. For example, all those magazines with pictures of celebrities and their cellulite falling out of taxis and showing their vaginas – once you've seen one, you've seen them all.

SO SAY GOODBYE TO *HELLO!* OR...

If you're finding it difficult to wean yourself off celebrity mags, then why not choose the longest checkout queue when you do your weekly shop? With any luck by the time it's your turn to be served, you will have read all you need to read in this week's *Hello!* and therefore you won't need to buy it. Money saved £2 x 50: £100 per annum. Well done.

OTHER SUPERMARKET ITEMS THAT YOU DON'T REALLY NEED

- **Antibacterial wipes** – just wash your hands.
- **Plug-in air-fresheners** – just open a window, or get him to light a match after he's been.
- **Fabric conditioner** – how soppy do you have to be?
- **Pak choi** – what's wrong with cabbage?
- **Chocolate cake** – it's not your birthday.
- **Extra-virgin olive oil** – listen, you're either a virgin or you're not a virgin; you can't be a bit of a virgin, and neither can you be 'extra-virgin'.
- **Cigarettes** – give up. You have to; what's the point in paying someone to kill you? You've probably got a friend or relative who would kill you for free.

-  **Space-age dishwasher tablets** – for some reason, the manufacturers like to make out that these are so cutting edge they have to be packaged like mercury. The rule of dishwashers is that nothing works all that well and that seven times out of ten you'll have to put at least three items back in to be rewashed.
- **Expensive shampoo** from a fancy hairdressing salon – unless your hair really is worth it, washing-up liquid will do the job just as well.
- **Sweets** – just grow up.

DON'T STOP BUYING

Those bags of salad, all washed and ready to serve – fiendishly expensive, yes, *but* at least you will eat the stuff, which is better than letting it go off in the salad tray, which is exactly what happens to any veg or salad stuff that needs a thorough rinsing before eating.

MORE TIPS FOR SHOPPING AT SUPERMARKETS

- The stuff that has the longest shelf life is always right at the back.
- If you want to know where something is, ask a female assistant in her 50s; that seventeen-year-old lad won't know. The other day I asked one if he knew the whereabouts of pumpernickel and he looked at me as if I was mad.
- Only buy two-for-one if you like whatever it is that's on offer.
- Yes, you will need some more loo roll; some things are not luxuries.

SPECIAL OFFERS AND HOW TO MAKE THE MOST OF THEM

M&S sometimes do a special 'Dine in for £10' offer for two (a main, side, pudding and bottle of wine, all for a tenner). This is great, but don't feel you need to share it with a partner. My friend divorced Debbie (not her real name) buys these meals and shares them not with her husband, who buggered off years ago, but with her ten-year-old son. Hoorah – she gets the bottle of wine all to herself.

NOTHING
SHRINKS
MORE THAN
SPINACH

(APART FROM CASHMERE ON A BOIL-WASH)

More SHOPPING RULES

CARPETS

Never buy a cream carpet. This is all I have to say on the subject.

SECOND-HAND CARS

Second-hand-car dealers have dreadful reputations. This is because they're all big fat liars who want to relieve you of your hard-earned cash in exchange for some old heap of rubbish.

BOOKS

Beware: make sure you don't buy the same book you read ages ago because the bloody publishers have repackaged it with a different cover.

ANOTHER EXPENSIVE MISTAKE

The wrong sort of ink cartridge for your computer. Trouble is, you always rip open the packaging before you realise what you've done – again!

FINALLY, A WORD OF WARNING ABOUT ONLINE SHOPPING

The trouble with online shopping is that you can buy anything from anywhere at any time of the day.

This is dangerous, as one of the good things about shops is that they are shut when you come out of the pub at 11 p.m. In the old days the only thing you could waste your money on post-midnight was some kind of greasy fast-food snack and a night bus in the wrong direction. Not any more – these days you stagger home, boot up the old Dell, feel a bit like treating yourself and the next thing you know you've bought that Mulberry bag, a pair of earrings a bit like Rihanna was wearing in this week's *Grazia* and some diet pills from India.

Obviously the only sensible solution is to leave your purse on the pub table. (Remove all your cash first.) Yes, it will be a bore having to cancel all your cards and wait for new ones to arrive through the post, but just think what damage you could have done with those cards if you'd managed to get them safely home. If a friend notices and runs after you with the purse, for God's sake don't hesitate – chuck your cards down the drain or post them through a letterbox; just get rid of them.

 REMEMBER, SHOP SENSIBLY – SHOP SOBER. DON'T DRINK AND SHOP.

HOW TO GET ABOUT ON A SHOESTRING*

SHANKS'S PONY†

Walking is obviously the cheapest form of transport, but it's quite impractical. Say, for example, you live in Leicester and you have to get to Swindon for a 2 p.m. meeting – walking there isn't going to work and no one is going to be particularly impressed when you turn up four days late.

CYCLING

This is a great way to get around in the summer if you live somewhere nice and flat/if you're quite fit and don't stand a chance of dropping down dead/if you don't mind developing massive calves/if you have time to shower when you get into work all sweaty from cycling/if you work somewhere that has a shower/more specifically, if you work somewhere that has a shower that's not going to give you legionnaires' disease/if you've got a decent lock/if you don't get scared at the prospect of being caught in the suction zone of a bendy bus/if you know what to do at the big, scary roundabout/and, most importantly, if you have hair that can deal with wearing a safety helmet without looking stupid for the rest of the day.

Otherwise cycling is an absolute nightmare.

----

* You can't: a shoestring is not a practical mode of transport. Ha, ha. (This is the sort of joke that used to be funny. Thank Christ we've moved on.)

† This, as we all know, is a euphemism for walking, even though it sounds like it should be a euphemism for something much ruder – like a slightly illegal sex act.

DRIVING

In the old days getting a car was something to aspire to. Basically, all young men wanted was a set of wheels that were smarter, faster and more powerful than their mates'. This is no longer the case – nowadays it's all about downsizing our cars to the smallest, slowest, least gas-guzzling model we can find. Preferably one of those little electric cars, a bit like Noddy used to drive.

All this is great for the planet, but it's given young men absolutely nothing to aim for, which is why half of them do nothing but lie in bed. Let's face it, they haven't got much to get up for, not when all they've got to drive is a little hybrid that has as much poke as a motorised shopping trolley and can only get up that big hill if the wind's behind it and they haven't got too much shopping in the boot.

WHY NOT CAR-SHARE?

Car-sharing is a great idea. Make sure you share with that bloke down the road who drives a Jensen Interceptor.

WARNING
DRIVING FURTHER TO GET CHEAP PETROL DOESN'T REALLY MAKE SENSE.

GUILT-FREE DRIVING

Make sure you use your car for something else:

- **A PORTABLE RABBIT HUTCH**
- **TO TRANSPORT OLD CLOTHES** and heavy unwanted items to a charity shop

- **TO TAKE YOUR OLD MUM OR A NEIGHBOUR TO HOSPITAL.** Let's face it, you can't put your old mum on the handlebars of a bike and cycle her to the Warfarin clinic.*
- **FOR DELIVERING LEAFLETS** on behalf of the Green Party.

While you are driving, you can also keep an eye out for your neighbour's dog, which went missing recently. You might be wasting precious resources, but you are also playing your part in the local community – make sure you don't run it over while you're looking for it.

BUSES AND COACHES ARE THE CHEAPEST FORM OF TRANSPORT

Unfortunately, they can also be full of the cheapest form of life. Avoid coaches unless you are a student and would rather spend your money on vodka shots than transport, or you're very old and don't care where you're going or how long it takes provided you've got a nice word search.

Of course, travelling by coach in a foreign country is somehow exotic. You always think you're going to meet some sexy cowboy on a Greyhound in the States, which isn't likely when you're on a National Express from Dudley to Wolverhampton.

Big, red buses in London are still the best way of getting about and seeing the capital. Unfortunately, they are also incredibly confusing and impossible to work out unless you've lived in the city for at least five years and know your Parsons Green from your Elmers End.

Country buses are just as bewildering and you might have to wait till a week on Wednesday to catch one, so make sure you've got a good book with you. Waiting for country buses is behind 99 per cent of vandalism in rural areas. People get so bored with waiting for the stupid bus that in the end the only thing they can do to stop themselves from going mad is to set fire to something or scribble some stupid graffiti, and who can blame them?

----

* Warfarin is a drug they use to thin the blood of heart patients – I've done my homework.

TRAINS

OK, the way trains are run in this country is more complicated than an entire box set of *Heroes* (a ridiculously convoluted American superheroes telly import). There is no rhyme or reason why certain trains from certain places at certain times should cost 133 times as much as the same journey taken three days later, but they do.

Facts

(1) **More people cry on trains** than any other mode of transport. This is because they have been found guilty of carrying the wrong sort of ticket and therefore must fork out for a full-price ticket (£320, thank you), even if they are 87 and can't see what's on the ticket because they have cataracts thicker than a shag-pile carpet.

(2) **You have to have a heart of stone** to be the sort of guard who implements these stupid rules – these bastards make London traffic wardens look like Hannah Montana. Do not marry one.

Unfortunately, we are all held to ransom by these wicked train operators, and instead of turning our backs on the thieving robbers, we pay into their disgusting coffers because the alternative is to spend the rest of our lives on the bloody coach.

PLANES

One of the great side effects of the increasingly popular green movement is that you can pretend that the reason you're not holidaying somewhere exotic is not because you can't afford the air fare, but because your conscience won't allow your carbon footprint to leave big stamp marks all over the sky. Ha! In reality, if you won the lottery, you'd be on the next available first-class flight to Mauritius. In fact, sod it – you'd hire your own private jet.

OTHER CHEAP MODES OF TRANSPORT

These include:
- **LIFT-CADGING** (but only with people you know, like your dad)
- **SCOOTERING**
- **ROLLER-BLADING**

MANNERS DON'T COST ANYTHING

Let's fine people who don't use them. Manners maketh man, so said William of Wykeham – this is the motto of Winchester School and New College, Oxford. Personally, I would add, 'and he should be able to drive'.

The trouble with this country today is that manners have gone completely out of fashion, and it's not just the everyday niceties that people can't be bothered with. They can't even be bothered to indicate when they want to turn left or right any more, which isn't just rude, it's dangerous. How come we got too cool for indicators?

Well, enough is enough. It's time to stem the tide of bad manners and drag Great Britain back into the land of the P&Q. So for starters, if we all refuse to pay for anything until the shop assistant has said 'please', this country would be a better place. Of course, the shopkeeper must retain the right to keep the purchased item on their side of the counter until we have thanked them for the transaction. Only then should the goods change hands.

And remember, it's 'Please may I have... ?', not 'Can I get... ?' If you want to get it, you can get it yourself.

FOR MEN

- **No leering** at fifteen-year-old girls who happen to be busty.
- **However, whistling at women over 40** on a nice summer's day when they're looking trim in that new linen dress is to be encouraged.
- **No toplessness** unless you are completely convinced it's a sight worth seeing, in which case, top off; it's your duty.
- **Doffing your hat** – this doesn't work with baseball caps; the correct 'good-manners hat' is the trilby. Hats should be doffed at ladies, if you can find any.
- **Walking on the outside of the pavement.** Traditionally men did this to prevent their female companion being splashed by passing motorists. I say bring this back, fellas, unless your coat is more expensive than hers, in which case shove her to the outside.

FOR WOMEN

🐾 **No wobbling down the street** after dark with your bosoms out just because it's Elaine's 50th and she's had a rubbish time ever since Michael went off with that Polish tart.

🐾 **Only ever fart in secret.** Honestly, in the olden days men had no idea that women let off!!!!!

🐾 **Don't slag your best friend's husband off** until the decree nisi has come through.

🐾 **If you've been to bed with a man** and he's made a lot of effort to please you, don't forget to say, 'Thank you very much for having me.' Even if you never intend to see him again.

🐾 **When a young man offers you his seat** on a crowded train, try and be grateful. Take the seat. Do not punch him in the face.

SPORTS MANNERS

We need to do something to stop footballers spitting, so from now on any footballer who spits on the pitch should have his legs amputated at the knee.

GIFT MANNERS

No thank-you letter = no Christmas present next year. Simple.

STREET MANNERS

👟 No gobbing.

👟 No graffiti (unless your name is Banksy).

👟 No mugging old ladies.

👟 No littering.

👟 No putting chewing gum on park benches.

👟 No pretending your dog hasn't done a great big shit.

👟 No weeing against lamp-posts/in phone boxes/in corners/in multi-storey car parks – especially during daylight hours.

👟 No throwing salad out of a kebab – you don't want anyone breaking a hip because they've slipped on your unwanted coleslaw.

👟 No stopping suddenly on a busy street and causing a pedestrian pile-up.

PUBLIC TRANSPORT MANNERS

☞ TEENAGERS, KEEP YOUR CRAPPY MUSIC TO YOURSELF OR SUFFER THE CONSEQUENCES. Teenagers who play loud music on public transport should be made to attend the Last Night of the Proms and be forced to listen to music they can't stand at full volume.

☞ NO TALKING TO YOUR MATES ON YOUR MOBILE IN A TEDIOUS FASHION. However, if the gossip is juicy, then do share, but at least have the consideration of filling us in on the background story. For example, 'I'm just talking to Jenna, who is so, like, late with her period. Only she just can't be pregnant 'cos, like, the only bloke she's had sex with in, like, weeks has been Jimmy B. and he is so, like, Kyra's boyfriend and Kyra don't know nothing. Only, soon as I get off talking to Jenna, I am so going to ring Kyra and tell her.' This is the sort of mobile-phone eavesdropping sesh that is worth missing a stop for.

☞ IF YOU FINISH A MAGAZINE ON THE BUS, DON'T JUST CHUCK IT ON THE FLOOR; OFFER IT TO YOUR FELLOW TRAVELLERS. Similarly, if you have just finished *War and Peace*, then why not offer that around?

☞ YOUNG MEN, IF YOU DON'T GET UP FOR THAT MIDDLE-AGED WOMAN, DON'T BE SURPRISED IF SHE PRETENDS TO LOSE HER BALANCE AND ACCIDENTALLY ON PURPOSE ENDS UP SITTING ON YOUR KNEE. You will be even more embarrassed if you inadvertently get an erection.

SOME OTHER SIMPLE RULES

☞ NO FARTING

☞ NO FEET ON SEATS

☞ NO PUTTING YOUR SHOPPING ON THE SEAT NEXT TO YOU. The bus might get busy, so shopping on the floor.

☞ NO TALKING OUT LOUD TO YOURSELF. It makes other passengers nervous.

☞ NO WIPING BOGIES UNDER THE SEAT

TALK
IS
CHEAP

but mobile-phone bills are expensive !

Table Manners

We really need to bring back table manners before people forget what tables were actually invented for. Just to remind you, here is a handy guide to setting a table, complete with napkins (serviettes are common):

- **Remember,** knives on the right; forks on the left; pudding spoons across the top with the bowl of the spoon nearest to the fork; soup spoons to the outside of the knife; napkins to the left of the fork. If it's a fancy do, work from the outside in, and don't take a swig from the finger bowl.
- **Cutlery** is to be encouraged. Proper use of knife, fork and spoon should be practised at all times. If we don't continue to use cutlery, then our knife, fork and spoon skills are going to disappear and some day in the not-too-distant future, people will only know how to eat with their fingers out of polystyrene containers and the entire nation will be covered from head to food in tomato sauce.
- **Knives** should not be held like a pen; you are eating, not writing. They are also cutting implements; cutting should be done as if you are sawing something and not just pulling at it.
- **Peas** should be squashed up against the back of the fork until you are down to the last three – then one last shovel is permitted.
- **Soup** spoons should be dragged outwards across the bowl, which should be tipped away from you. There is no practical reason for this as far as we can see; it's just one of those things that differentiate us from pigs.

FURTHER TABLE MANNERS

- **Wash your hands** before coming to the table.
- **Do not blow** your nose on your napkin.
- **Bring your food to your mouth,** not your mouth to your food.
- **Serve others** before serving yourself.
- **No texting at the table.** Turn mobile phones off.
- **Remember, elbows off the table,** or, as my grandmother would say, 'All joints on the table will be carved.' A threat my cousin Eliza didn't take seriously. What a Christmas lunch that was! Eliza now has no elbows and is a complete liability in the January sales.
- **Do not lick the plate,** unless you're abroad – they eat like pigs over there.

'CONVERSATION'
A FUN GAME FOR ALL THE FAMILY

It is bad manners to watch television while eating a meal – I know this might come as a bit of a shock, but honestly it's true. Maybe the government should introduce a TV curfew at least once a week between the hours of 6 and 8 p.m. This might encourage families to sit together and have a conversation. To help you get started here's a fun game for all the family that lasts anything from a minute to whenever someone goes flouncing off and slams a door. For two or more players.

THE RULES

(1) It's important to sit far away from each other to make pulling hair impossible.

(2) First things first, get a tape measure and measure a safe distance between the participants (members of the family).

(3) Use a die to decide who gets to start the conversation. The person with the highest score after three throws of the die begins. Anyone who argues with this rule should be disqualified from the game and forgo their meal.

(4) All players have to ask at least one question and answer another politely before being served any food.

(5) Handy question cards can be placed in a bowl in the middle of the table. These might help the conversation to flow. The questions would range from simple general-knowledge questions such as 'What did you do today?' to more in-depth questions such as 'What's the point in going on?' and 'Do you think happiness really exists?'

(6) Players are not allowed to answer a question by grunting or shrugging.

(7) Players who are new to the game should take turns in speaking. As with all good games, turns should be taken in an anticlockwise direction. Once players have become more experienced, they will be able to do what is known as 'interject'. Eventually they will be able to hold a game of Conversation without having to wait for their go.

(8) The most reasonable member of the family should be appointed referee. This person should have a whistle, which they can blow as a warning to players that the conversation has moved on to dangerous territory – for example, say a seventeen-year-old girl says to her fifteen-year-old sister, 'What have you done with my purple shirt, you fat cow?'

(9) Any player who incurs three conversational red cards (whistles) should be removed from the table, locked out of the house, if necessary, and not given any pudding.

(10) Advanced players of Conversation occasionally find they enjoy playing the game so much that they forget to turn the telly on, but this is very rare.

FALSE ECONOMY

Obviously we're keen to cut all sorts of financial corners whenever and wherever we can, but some monetary short cuts just aren't worth the bother. For example...

Cutting Your Own Hair

Leave your fringe alone. Cutting your own fringe will only lead to lowering your chances of promotion or sexual favours or both. You'll get carried away trying to level it off and invariably it will end up too short, making you look like a missionary or a half-wit.

Home perming is also a very bad idea and will take months of wearing hats until you feel confident enough to show your head in public again – not worth it. Ditto home bleaching – when it falls out, you will have no one to blame but yourself. Remember, if you go to a salon and they muck up your hair, you can at least pretend that you are a bride-to-be and sue them for ruining the photos.

Walking Home Late at Night Instead of Getting a Cab

Don't be so silly. Chances are, you could get mugged. Now, that's not economically sound, is it? You might have saved 20 quid on a cab fare, but how much is replacing your handbag, phone, make-up bag (not to mention having to have your locks changed) going to cost you? A lot, that's how much.

Get a cab. You know it makes sense – unless there's a bus going your way, which actually makes more sense, unless of course a tramp sitting next to you throws up on your coat, in which case getting the cab is going to be cheaper than buying a new coat! Hmm, decisions, decisions!

Hitch-Hiking

Some things were always a silly idea. There's nothing clever about saving a few quid when you're lying face down strangled in a ditch.

Rewiring Your Own House

You bloody fool, you don't know what you're doing.

Digging Your Own Pond/Swimming Pool

Ditto. You might save money, but your marriage will break down. For God's sake, call in the experts.*

Going Home to Live With Your Parents

It might be cheap, but they will drive you insane. Within days you will be a shadow of your former self. If you stay much longer, you will lose the ability to cut up your own food and tie your own shoelaces. Get out while you can, otherwise you know what will happen... Your aged mum will 'have a fall', thereby rendering escape impossible. You *have* to stay and look after her. Bingo – you are now trapped in some Beckett-like scenario of mutual dependency and loathing.

The thing about parents is that they like to think that you are a successful, functioning adult – this is an act you can probably pull off as long as you don't see them all that often. If you limit your visits to, say, three a year, you will have time to get your story straight, perhaps hire a decent car, wife/husband and kids, just to keep the image up. If, on the other hand, you end up living with your parents, they will soon realise that what they have bred is a spineless loser and their disappointment will be so great that they will write you out of the will.

Remember, with relatives, it's safest to keep your distance. Families are a bit like cars cruising down the motorway – if you get too close, it can end up in a great big pile-up with everyone blaming each other and lots of tears.

---

* We cannot guarantee that calling in the experts will save your marriage. Quite a lot of women find experts really attractive, especially compared to their incompetent husbands, and will therefore have sex with them (the experts, not the incompetent husbands. Plumbers score most highly in this area.)

MORE
FALSE ECONOMY

SOMETIMES IT'S CHEAPER IN THE LONG RUN TO GET YOUR PURSE OUT, ESPECIALLY IF NOT FORKING OUT FOR SOMETHING THAT MIGHT KILL YOU
(OR WORSE, MAKE YOU LOOK REALLY STUPID)

DON'T BUY

* **REALLY CHEAP MEAT** from a market stall that looks like it's owned by the League of Gentlemen – if it really is chicken, why do the bones look like babies' knees?

* **DVDs** from a market stall – they will jam.

* **JAM** from a DVD stall – it's not right.

* **LUNCH** from a gastro pub – this will be a rip-off on a plate.

* **SKIS**, on the premise that you won't ever have to waste money hiring them – what will inevitably happen is that, even with your very own skis, you will hate skiing so much that you will have to sell the stupid fucking skis and that ridiculous pod thing for carrying them on top of the car at a silly loss.

* **GOLF CLUBS** – see above.

* **AN ITEM OF CLOTHING** that isn't quite right but will probably look great once you've shortened it and changed the buttons – you never will. Fact: any alterations that require the threading of a needle will never get done.

* **A PAIR OF** size 12 trousers when you are a size 16 but 'on a diet' – not being able to get into these trousers will make you so depressed that you will comfort-binge and balloon to a size 18, which means not only can you not fit into the size-12 trousers, you can't fit into anything else either.

* **A HOUSE** on the cheap because it has been repossessed – you might have got a bargain, but at what price? Every time you set foot in your cut-price house, you

will hear the walls sob a little, feel the floorboards groan. Maybe you will find a tiny shoe fit only for a Barbie that has fallen through a crack in the floorboards. And what's that in the bathroom cabinet? An empty Valium packet – yet another reminder of the once-happy family who were wrenched from their home so that you could leap in and take advantage of their sad situation. And where might that family be now? On the street? In a shelter? Or, worse, living with his mother in Swansea? Guilt will begin to keep you awake at night; exhaustion will set in; you will be reprimanded for poor timekeeping at work; eventually you will lose your job; you won't be able to make the mortgage repayments. Soon it won't be friends knocking on the door; it'll be the bailiffs. This is modern-day karma.

* **A RACEHORSE** – there is no guarantee that it will win the Grand National and make you rich. Instead, get something small and inexpensive, like a hamster. (Maybe you could race the hamster.)
* **CHEAP TOILET PAPER** – your fingers will only go through it. Never again.
* **FAKE SELLOTAPE,** which is really just some vaguely sticky see-through tape that isn't a patch on the real thing. A bit like a poor-quality Dr Who – for example Colin Baker.

OTHER CHEAP THINGS THAT AREN'T WORTH SPENDING YOUR MONEY ON

* **TINNED CARROTS** – they are disgusting.
* **FAKE** Gucci or Louis Vuitton handbags from a South London market – these are just naff and rubbish.
* **GOLD EARRINGS** that aren't gold and turn your ears green.
* **A RAIN MAC** that isn't waterproof.
* **KNICKERS** that don't have a cotton gusset.
* **BATTERIES** by a company you've never heard of.

* **STALE BISCUITS.**
* **ANY OF** the following DVDs: *Lesbian Vampire Killers* (aka Horne and Corden's biggest mistake); *Fat Slags* (what was Sophie Thompson thinking of?); *Sex Lives of the Potato Men* (so much talent in so much crap); *Basic Instinct 2* (why?); *Swept Away* (the Madonna thing that really tanked); and basically (as a general rule of thumb) most films starring Matthew Perry who used to be in *Friends*.

Some Ideas to Make You Feel Richer

The thing about really posh people is that even when they don't have any money, they manage to be poor with style. This is better than being poor with no style – i.e. sitting in an unfurnished squat, watching *The Jeremy Kyle Show* on a TV that you haven't paid a licence fee for while eating supermarket-brand cat food straight out of the tin.

Basically, there is a difference between being financially embarrassed and being skint. What we're after here is 'impoverished gentility'. Coming across as posh despite having absolutely no money will open doors to places where there might be finger food and champagne.

Sleeping Your Way into High Society

Forget your football players, girls. Unless you're a busty blonde with massive tits or a dusky maiden with massive tits, you've got no chance. Why don't you try for a polo player instead? They've got proper money, and because they went to an all-boys boarding school, you won't necessarily need massive tits; the fact that you are female will be novelty enough.

Oh yes, and remember, if anyone mentions water polo, it doesn't involve horses. I thought it did and consequently found the sport rather disappointing.

Your Address

Not everyone can afford to live in Kensington and Chelsea. The only way mere mortals can afford a posh postcode is if they're really lucky and have managed to nab one of those Peabody council jobbies a stone's throw from the King's Road. Chances are, with the current property fiasco, it's going to be years before you can move somewhere nicer in a better area, but who says you need to move house to have a change of address?

Feel better about where you live simply by giving your house a name rather than a number. This will instantly make your house sound a lot more expensive – for example, changing your address from 15 Sydenham Road to Flitcroft Hall will cheer you up no end. OK, so it might be the same two-bedroom maisonette on a busy dual carriageway that smells of feet and kippers, but so what?

SOME SUGGESTIONS FOR NAMES

The Maltings

Little Orchards

Trelawney

Seven Chimneys

Pitlochry Towers

Minchin Hall

If you need more house-name ideas, just flick through some old Agatha Christies for inspiration.

WHY NOT GIVE ALL YOUR CHILDREN NAMES THAT HAVE THE SAME INITIAL?

You'll save a fortune on Cash's nametapes – for example, Tamarind, Tarquin and Tabouleh.

Many houses take their name from their physical attributes – for example, a house might be called Silver Birches thanks to its abundance of said tree. However, this is not law and you can call your house whatever you like. In fact, if you live on the thirteenth floor of a South London high-rise, there is no reason why you can't call your flat Rose Cottage. Remember, though, no name at all is sometimes preferable to any old name and honesty is not the best policy. For instance, do not call your house Dog-Shit Corner, even if it is.

Born-Again Posh

You don't have to be born with a silver spoon in your mouth to sound like you were. For best results, practise talking with a large silver spoon in your mouth. Once you've got the hang of it, remove the spoon and:

* Tell people you studied history at Magdalen College, Oxford. Just don't let yourself down by mispronouncing Magdalen (maudlin).

* Refer to your parents as 'Mummy and Daddy'. Only really rich people do this. You will sound like a twat, but you will sound like a twat with money.

* Ask where the knives and forks are in McDonald's or request a finger bowl in KFC.

How to Look Like a Rich Person

Rich people are notoriously badly dressed; all you need is a jumper with loads of holes in it. This is because big old stately homes always have moths. Team with a pair of green wellies and a tortoiseshell Alice band and, hey presto, you look like an eccentric millionaire.

If you want to look like a member of the gentry, wear anything that looks like riding gear. A pair of jodhpurs, a woolly and some wellies is a pretty cheap get-up, but the connotations – i.e. that you have your own horse – reek of money. Accessorise this look with manure squidged under the heel of your wellington boots and some hay in your hair. Carry a riding crop and say things like, 'I'm awfully worried about Blaze. Her right hock seems terribly inflamed.'

Be flamboyant – buy some velvet curtains from a second-hand shop and drape them around you, smoke small cigars and wear dramatic eye make-up; everyone will think you are a Polish heiress.

Make friends with Jerry Hall and borrow her stuff. (Tricky if you're five foot and a size 16.)

Affect Posh Connections

Have a fictional aunt and call her something eccentric like Great-Aunt Trilby. Hint that this woman is madly rich, childless, utterly bonkers and living on an unpronounceable estate in

THE IMPORTANCE OF NAMES

Change your name to Guinness or Kashoggi or Getty, wear dark glasses and scurry out of posh restaurants via the kitchen exit. People might think you are a celebrity, rather than someone who actually works in the kitchen. (Tip: take your pinny off.)

Make sure you give your mutt a classy name. Greek names are good – they suggest you know your classics, and if all you can afford are a couple of hamsters, then why not call them Dido and Aeneas?* Ditto take care when naming your children. You can live up the arse end of Arsenal but as long as you call your children Araminta and Tarquin, no one would ever guess.

* Choose your dog with care: a chocolate-brown Labrador barks 'class'; a foul, mean-eyed Staffy doesn't.

Ireland. Drop sentences into the conversation such as 'Of course it was Great-Aunt Trilby who taught me to fish.' This will conjure up a childhood of privilege and the possibility that one day you might inherit a good deal of land complete with fishing rights.

OTHER FOODIE THINGS MUCH LOVED BY THE POSH

- 👑 **BREAD-AND-BUTTER PUDDING** 'like Nanny used to make'
- 👑 **RICE PUDDING** with skin on top
- 👑 **VENISON***
- 👑 **GROUSE**
- 👑 **KEDGEREE** (for breakfast)
- 👑 **KIPPERS** (ditto)
- 👑 **SMOKED SALMON†** and scrambled eggs (ditto).

* The pronunciation of venison: always make sure the 's' sounds like a 'z'; this will make you sound like someone who eats venison a lot.

† Basically, eating fish first thing in the morning is a sign of loadedness; however, this does not include fish fingers.

Posh Hobbies

Know how to do some Scottish dancing. All posh people have at some point been drilled in the art of the eightsome reel and the gay Gordons; knowing how to do a few Scottish dances smacks of being the kind of person who has attended a lot of weekend house parties with ballrooms.

Eat Like The Gentry

Learn how to eat oysters: only the upper classes have genuine oyster-friendly taste buds. This comes from having developed cast-iron gag reflexes at boarding school, where years of vile food have made them immune to the true repulsiveness of the bivalve.

Remember, if You Want to Be Posh, It's...

- **Earl Grey** not Tetley
- **mayonnaise** not salad cream
- **olive oil** not lard
- **tweed** not Lycra
- **The Times** not the *Express*
- **Sainsbury's** not Lidl
- **Radio 4** not Magic FM
- **Kettle Chips** not Walkers
- **pants** not G-strings
- **Ikea** not DFS
- **goujons** not chicken nuggets
- **Boots** not Superdrug
- **sofa** not settee
- **fountain pens** not biros
- **Stilton** not cheese strings
- **Peter Jones** not Debenhams
- **natural nails** not French polishes
- **pearl earrings** not belly-button rings
- **point-to-point** not pole-dancing
- **rugby** not football
- **sherry** not Smirnoff Ice
- **Debrett's** not Facebook
- **cashmere, even if it's riddled with moth holes,** not acrylic
- **teacups** and saucers not mugs
- **Freeview** not Sky
- **The Antiques Roadshow** not *Flog It!*
- **AA roadmaps** not sat nav
- **horse blankets** not yoga mats
- **film** not digital cameras
- **heirlooms** not bling.

PHONES FOR U AND NOT U

Pretending to be posher than you are gives you the excuse not to have to keep up with the latest phone fad. Really posh people don't care about things like that. In fact, the posher the person, the more antiquated the Nokia. Sport your knackered Nokia with pride and just remember when you answer it to yell really poshly.

BASIC ENTREPRENEURIALISM
SKILL SWAPPING

Have you got what it takes to be a businessman or -woman? Even if the answer is 'no', why not have a go anyway? Who knows, you might accidentally stumble on a good idea. For example, not everything needs to cost cash; you can always set up your own non-currency locally by doing away with money altogether and skill-swapping instead. Think about what you can offer and what your neighbours could do with. Maybe you are great at hanging wallpaper – you could swap a day's worth of wallpaper hanging for a day's worth of gardening.

Don't automatically leap to the conclusion that you and your friends can't do anything; everyone can do something – just use your imagination! Say, for example, your best chum is really great at giving blow-jobs. Why not borrow her for your partner's birthday and in return (because you are more intellectual) read her book-club book and make notes for her?

SOME SKILLS YOU MIGHT BE ABLE TO SWAP

* **Killing nits** – some people really enjoy squashing nits in an infested child's hair.

* **Cleaning the teeth of toddlers** who don't want to open their mouth.

* **Folding jumpers** – if you need to gain experience, why not train yourself up by getting a Saturday job in Gap?

* **Tuning a Freeview box** – preferably to get more channels than have actually been paid for.

* **Downloading software** on to computers – this is not something you should pretend you can do.

* **Finding things** – again, a skill born of age and experience. Mums know where stuff is because no one else in the house has a clue,

and anyway, mums have got eyes in the back of their head, so have the advantage of a handy set of secondary optical organs.

* **Spreading malicious gossip** – dead easy, particularly for women of a certain age, who are such naturals they sometimes do it without even realising.
* **Cleaning out kitchen drawers** – anyone can tidy the knives and forks up, but we mean a proper clean-out, including getting rid of all that cruddy stuff at the bottom of the drawer.
* **Remembering birthdays,** buying cards and posting them – some people are just more organised than others. These are the people who put important dates in their diary, know where their diary is, check their diary and always have a set of stamps in the stamp compartment of their purse. Is this you?
* **Identifying birds** (but only the obvious ones) – robins are dead easy, as they have the giveaway red breast; other easy ones include blue tits (no, they don't have blue tits like lady Smurfs – ha, ha) and magpies.
* **Looking for lost cats** – and not just pretending to look for the stupid thing.
* **Watching telly** without talking – maybe you could supply your own muzzle, or simply put a sock in your mouth.
* **Sewing on nametapes** – neatly, so that they stay on.
* **Lighting fires** (not dangerous, arson-type fires, just legal, indoor fires) with kindling and proper log construction.
* **Burying dead animals** (complete with own spade) – to qualify for this job, all you need is a complete lack of squeamishness and the strength to dig whatever size hole is required.
* **Doing year-eleven physics homework** – but only if you think you can.

WHAT YOU COULD SWAP THESE SKILLS FOR

* some homemade ice cream
* Johnny Depp's autograph
* a box set of *Peep Show*
* a jumper
* an exercise bike
* some French lessons
* a recipe for a really nice cake
* the lending of some salopettes
* a lift to Newcastle
* the wheels fixing on a broken skateboard.

The possibilities are endless.

ADVANCED ENTREPRENEURIALISM

SOME BUSINESSES YOU CAN SET UP FROM HOME

Of course, it's just a small step from offering swapping services to setting up your own business at home. There are all sorts of things that you can operate from the comfort of your own home. Now that we've all got the Internet (apart from my mum), you can advertise whatever service you want to offer on the World Wide Web and wait for the jobs to come rolling in.

THE SHOULDER-TO-CRY-ON SERVICE

Offer this service for women who have been dumped and have run out of friends to bleat on about it to. Get yourself a bike and offer to cycle anywhere within a half-mile radius of where you live (unless any big hills are involved), taking succour, red wine and chocolate round to anyone who finds themselves weepy and boyfriendless on a Friday night.

THE DELUXE SHOULDER-TO-CRY-ON SERVICE

Would include the standard red wine and chocolates, plus a 30-minute karaoke session complete with 'I Will Survive' and 'Sisters Are Doin' It for Themselves', plus a one-hour rant about why the low-down two-timing ex was a no-good waste of time and how the client is better off without him (even if they're inconsolably lonely).

GRANDMA/PA FOR THE AFTERNOON

Lots of children have grandparents who live too far away – say in Australia or Wales – for them to visit regularly. For these children, the mind-numbing boredom of having to visit an elderly relative is something they might never have to endure. Well, now they can, with fake granny visits!!! If you're over 60, why not set yourself up as a proper old-fashioned nana, complete with doilies and biscuits that taste like they've been kept in a hamster's cage? For a fee, you can 'entertain' kiddies who would rather be anywhere else. Make them do a jigsaw or hold massive skeins of wool for hours on end while you rewind it into balls.

Perhaps if you have a partner, he could pretend to be Grandpa and go on endlessly about fly-fishing while smoking a pipe. Charge extra if you've got a greenhouse or a tool shed where the kids can be put to work doing some little jobs – maybe introduce them to the concept of weeding.

Give 21st-century kids a real flavour of what life was like when children couldn't just do what they pleased and visiting grandparents was compulsory.

THE SAFEKEEPING COMPANY

This home-based business would entail you keeping things safe for other people. For example, someone might have bought a bike for their son's twelfth birthday and they need to hide it somewhere safe until the actual day. (This is where you would come in.) For a small fee, you could keep the bike (or whatever) safe until that day came.

You could also open this service up to parents who are going away for the weekend and don't trust their idiot teenage children not to smash some expensive vases or break their Bang & Olufsen stereo.

CALLING ALL BRAINBOXES – ARE YOU FED UP WITH SITTING AT HOME ANSWERING LOADS OF QUESTIONS ON *UNIVERSITY CHALLENGE*? ARE YOU BORED WITH FEELING INTELLECTUALLY SUPERIOR BUT UTTERLY SKINT? THEN LET'S GET THOSE GREY CELLS OUT THERE AND EARNING.

Yes, here's a simple way of earning a few bob, cash in hand, and all you need do is pop out for a couple of hours at night. No, we don't mean you should become a prostitute; that's silly and dangerous and you could contract something very nasty that will make your downstairs area itch. No, instead of being a prostitute, why not form your own pub-quiz team? Not only will forming your own pub-quiz team keep the old brain ticking, it might just help keep the British pub alive. Their fate is in your hands. It's time to recruit.

STEP 1: CHOOSE YOUR TEAM

The first thing you need to do is to choose your team. Look around at your circle of friends. Are any of them clever? Remind yourself of their jobs. Barristers, doctors and teachers tend to be clever. Estate agents, media personalities and journalists tend to be cunning and not above cheating. Good – these people will help you win. Ideally your team should include a doctor, a magazine hack, a geography teacher, a history nut and someone who is perhaps a bit thick, as they'll answer all the questions on soap operas. Hmm, maybe that thick person is you? Gather your potential quizzers in your living room and practise a few typical pub-quiz rounds. It's useful at this point to have some other clever friends in reserve in case some of your potential candidates turn out to be a bit slower than anticipated.

STEP 2: CHOOSE A NAME

Once you've picked your boffins, it's important to choose a name for your team. This will cement a feeling of solidarity and hopefully stop members running off and joining other pub-quiz teams. Loyalty is vital.

SOME TEAM-NAME SUGGESTIONS

If you haven't got a very fertile imagination, here are some ideas for team names:

The Brainboxes

The Quizzers (not very good)

Gold-Star Brigade

THE CLEVER NOGGINS

STEP 3: PRACTISE

It's important that before you start competing, your team is match-fit, so a few dummy runs are a good idea.

SOME GENERAL-KNOWLEDGE Q&As THAT MIGHT COME IN HANDY

Ideally your chosen team of quizzers should be able to romp through these questions without breaking a sweat. (Answers upside down at the bottom of this page)

(1) What is the name of the condition that causes your extremities to go numb in cold weather?

(2) How many children in *The Sound of Music*?

(3) Who wrote *The Wind in the Willows*?

1. Frostbite 2. Seven 3. Kenneth Grahame

DOS AND DON'TS

JUST FOLLOW THESE BASIC DOS AND DON'TS AND YOU SHOULD BE ALL RIGHT:

DO **REMEMBER IT'S ALL IN THE PLANNING.** Why not blow up a map of your local area and plot all the pubs on the map known to hold regular quizzes? It might be that you live in an area that is saturated with pub quizzes and with careful planning you might be able to attend more than one quiz in an evening. Check what's on offer, though, as some pubs will have better prize money than others; some pubs might offer silly prizes that you don't want, like a large tin of ham.

DO **MAKE SURE YOU HAVE YOUR OWN SUPPLY OF PENCILS AND BIROS.** Being equipped will make you feel more efficient and give you confidence. This confidence can be very off-putting for other teams. Good – you already have the psychological advantage.

DO **AVOID ARRIVING EARLY, ESPECIALLY IF THE QUIZ IS BEING HELD IN A GASTRO PUB.** You will only want to order the crabcakes with mango and samphire, which will come to £17, or more if you add a cheeky glass of Sancerre. Novice, keep it real, keep it cheap – make yourself a sardine sandwich and eat it in the toilet. (Note: oily fish is well known for being good brain food.)

DO **TRY PUBS IN DIFFERENT AREAS.** Some places might be brainier than others. For example, you're likely to have an entirely different calibre of question in a pub in Hampstead compared to a pub in Salford. A Hampstead pub quiz would probably have questions like 'Which is the smelliest cheese?' and 'How many kilometres is Puglia from the airport?' Whereas in Salford you might get asked, 'What is David Beckham's middle name?'

DO **COME TO AN AGREEMENT ABOUT HOW YOU'RE GOING TO SPLIT THE WINNINGS.** Here's an idea: why not offer to keep the winnings in a large pot and then split the cash at the end of a six-month period? After five months you could always run away with the money, change your identity and start your life anew in a strange area.

DO **SORT OUT TRANSPORT.** Public transport can let you down and make you late for crucial quizzes, so a minibus is your best bet. You can probably pick one up for about £3,000. Maybe use a stencil and spray-paint the name of your team on the side of the minibus. This will look the business.

DON'T **DRINK.** It is a medically proven fact that alcohol makes you forget stuff. The more you drink, the more you forget. This is very bad if it is your duty to remember the chronological order of kings and queens through the ages. After two units of alcohol you will get muddled around the Middle Ages and probably forget Ethelred the Unready. Stick to cheap beverages like blackcurrant and soda.

DON'T **DRINK SO MUCH BLACKCURRANT AND SODA THAT YOU NEED TO KEEP POPPING TO THE LOO.** This will ruin your concentration and that of your team-mates.

DON'T **GET CARRIED AWAY ON A WAVE OF CELEBRATION IF YOU WIN.** There is always the danger that you will start splashing out on champagne and post-win Indian meals, which will get out of hand and cost you more than your winnings, especially if you get too drunk to drive the minibus and end up having to send your team home in a cab.

DON'T **CHEAT;** you will be banned for life.

DON'T **APPORTION BLAME.** However, if one person keeps letting the side down, just forget to pick him up in the minibus. After a couple of weeks he'll get the message – unless he really is incredibly thick.

DON'T **BE A SORE LOSER.** Sometimes it's not about who is the cleverest team; it's about one team knowing more answers than you. Yes, they probably cheated, but that's no reason to beat them up in the car park. Let it go. Tomorrow is another night and another quiz.

TO MASCOT OR NOT TO MASCOT?

This depends on how much you want the other teams to hate your guts: everyone hates teams with mascots. If you do decide to go for it, why not make your own mascot? How exotic this is is up to you. Maybe you're not artistically inclined, in which case why not draw a face on a paper bag?

A really good idea is to have a human mascot. Why not opt for a child genius? One of those weird kids who can answer all the tricky maths questions and can be fobbed off with some sweets rather than money. Of course, if your genius is very young, they might prove to be a bit of a liability – for example, falling asleep in the later rounds. Make sure this doesn't happen by pinching them awake.

BUDGET FUN 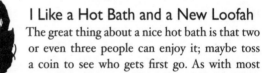for you

I Like a Hot Bath and a New Loofah

The great thing about a nice hot bath is that two or even three people can enjoy it; maybe toss a coin to see who gets first go. As with most things, preparation is the key to really enjoying a hot bath. Make sure you have a nice dry towel ready, a good book or magazine, maybe some biscuits and a glass of wine (not if it's morning, though – there's relaxing and there's being a pisshead).

I Like Doing Jigsaw Puzzles Even When I'm Not Ill

The trick here is to choose a jigsaw that's not too hard for you. I'm not suggesting you limit yourself to a four-piece wooden Spot the Dog number, but just don't do a really complicated jigsaw with loads of sky or boats in a harbour, as it might just push you over the edge and make you take up smoking again.

I Like a Nice Celebrity Chav Wedding in *Hello!*

Oh, is there anything guaranteed to make you feel more superior than a load of desperate D-listers done up like Disney 'princesses' especially when you can still see their tattoos peeking out? If you don't want to waste your own money on buying this rubbish, keep your beady eye on your neighbour's recycling bin. With any luck you can nick all her finished-with magazines and read her discarded post for added entertainment.

I Like a Pickled Onion That's Big Enough and Tangy Enough to Make My Eyes Water

Ooh, just thinking about this is making me dribble. The brownish ones in dark vinegar are the best; silverskins are for babies (not literally).

I Like Throwing Snails Over Next Door's Garden Wall

Just don't be surprised if they throw something they don't want back, like an unwanted cooker.

I Like Playing Scrabble With People Who Are Too Young to Realise That I'm Cheating

Basically, anyone under ten is a sucker for made-up words. Ha! The fools! Or should I say 'pliazxys? Yeah, get that on a triple word score and you've won.

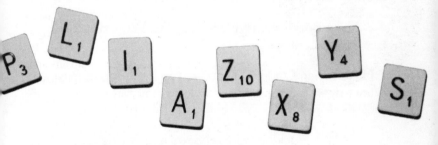

I Like Looking at the Clothes in *Grazia* and Playing 'If I Had to Buy a Pair of Shoes on This Page, Which Ones Would I Buy?'

Just don't get too disappointed when you look in your wardrobe for those purple suede boots you 'bought' only to find that there is a difference between buying something and imagining you've bought something.

I Like Bitching With a Friend About Another Friend Whom Neither of Us Likes Much

Ah... what it is to be a woman.

I Like Dipping My Finger Into a Brand-New Jar of Peanut Butter

Be careful who you admit this to; there is a fine line between harmless enjoyment and fetish.

I Like Bothering to Make a Coffee With Hot Milk

Like a latte, only cheaper.

I Like Trying On Hats That I've No Intention of Buying

When I say 'no intention of buying', make sure you don't accidentally walk out of the shop with one on your head and get arrested for shoplifting.

I Like Plucking My Eyebrows and Seeing How Juicy the Roots of the Hairs I Have Plucked Are by Holding Them Up to the Light

Possibly this is a 'hobby' it's best to keep quiet about.

I Like Clean Sheets and a Hot-Water Bottle

Just remember to screw the lid on the hot-water bottle as tightly as possible; there is nothing worse than waking up in lukewarm liquid. Well, actually there is – there's waking up soaked in your own urine, which is much worse, but you know what I mean.

I Like Mucking About in the Supermarket

This is a simple game that never loses its fun factor. All you do is move as many things on to the wrong shelf in Tesco as you can without arousing suspicion – for example, put some tampons in the middle of the cat-litter shelf. A little bit of chaos can go a long way and might just create a new position for your teenage son, who needs a Saturday job.

I Like Mucking About in Clothes Shops

This is a variation of the above. Just try on loads of things and then hand them back to the assistant inside out and back to front – that'll teach her for chewing gum and looking gormless. If she cheeks you, get her sacked. Good – there just might be a vacancy for your teenage daughter, who is in dire need of a Saturday job.

I Like an Afternoon Nap

Especially a secret one, taken when there's no one in the house, so you can pretend you were really busy doing something else. Ha, ha, ha.

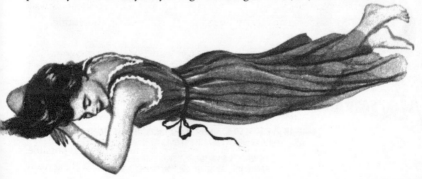

Also available: HOME, SWEET HOMELESS, IF WE CAN'T PAY THE MORTGAGE.

CLEANLINESS IS NEXT TO GODLINESS, BUT NOT IN THE DICTIONARY.

CHILDREN SHOULD BE SEEN AND NOT HEARD, UNLESS THEY'RE UNATTRACTIVE
AND CLEVER, IN WHICH CASE THEY SHOULD BE HEARD AND NOT SEEN.

PATIENCE IS A VIRTUE, BUT SWEARING IS MORE
SATISFYING, SO HURRY UP, YOU STUPID TWATS.

ADRENALINE JUNKIES

CHEAP THRILLS – DANGEROUS SPORTS THAT WON'T COST A PACKET

FORGET DIVING WITH SHARKS AND SNOWBOARDING.

Why not go SHOPLIFTING?

Guaranteed to get your blood pumping. No special gear required: no snorkel or wet suit; no bulky skis. All you need is a mac with big pockets and some trainers so you can run away from the store detective if necessary.

SHOPLIFTING MADE EASY WITH SPECIAL HOUR-LONG TRAINING COURSES:

- How to look nonchalant in the wines and spirits
- Getting rid of security tags (with your teeth)
- Running away. Know where to go with our 'Running Away and Hiding Behind Some Bins' Ordnance Survey maps.

YOUR POCKET GUIDE TO EXCUSES – FOR EXAMPLE:

- redundancy
- postnatal depression (women only)
- feelings of inadequacy (a brilliant excuse, as it covers all eventualities and is impossible to disprove).

The Chin Up Guide to
GATE-CRASHING

••••••••••••••••••••••••••••••••••••

Skint, bored and fed up with other people having a fantastic time while you stay at home night after night? Well, just because you're poor and unpopular doesn't mean that you should be socially disadvantaged. As we all know, there are several ways of getting into private clubs and parties: a) be invited; b) bribe your way in (do not, however, get so desperate that you are prepared to give a doorman a blow-job. There isn't a club in the world – not even in Essex – that is worth this); and c) gate-crash.

Yes, gate-crashing is much cooler than being on the guest list. Let's face it, we all need to let our hair down now and again, and parties can really cheer you up, especially if you're not paying for them. However, the trouble with being the type of person who never forks out for a party is that you can soon become the type of person who doesn't get invited to any parties.

Go on, check your mantelpiece. Is it crowded with gilt-edged invitations? No.

Now have a look in your diary. Does it say, 'Gill and Keith's fancy dress?' Thought not.

Don't despair – you don't have to be invited to a party to go to a party. All you need to know are the Chin Up rules to civilised gate-crashing.

CRASHING WITH DISCRIMINATION

Don't crash the wrong party. If you're over 50, don't bother crashing any parties that are dominated by teenagers. One of them will be sick on your shoes and there won't be anything to eat – you will also hate the music and someone will think you're an undercover drugs officer.

Similarly, if you're under 20, it's not cool to wander through a set of random French windows just outside Godalming and sit yourself down at Angela and

Rory's supper for twelve. Rory is celebrating his 44th birthday and he likes golf. All the talk around the table will be about golf, and no one will have any drugs, unless you count the Valium that's in that weird-looking woman's handbag. They will also expect you to join in conversations about recycling, private versus state schools and...golf.

Before setting off to gate-crash a party, try to decide what sort of party you'd like to crash. For example...

F OR THE BEST FREE BOOZE. Art galleries are good for free booze. Just walk up and down Cork Street in London on a Thursday night, which is the night for private views, and take your pick. It's best if you look arty: wear something velvet and a hat, and walk around saying, 'It's the subliminal visceral quality that makes my womb ache. Blah, blah...fishcakes.'

Experienced private-view crashers might manage six or seven galleries in a night. Hoorah – this is the arty freeloader's equivalent to a cost-effective pub crawl.

CHIN UP GUIDE TO GATE-CRASHING

FOR THE BEST FREE BOOZE

F OR THE BEST CANAPÉS. Aim for those traditional engagement bashes that only people who live in the country still have – you know, the sort of thing that *Country Life* send photographers to. It's probably worth taking a cheap train to Wiltshire and then scouting about for catering vans down gravel drives and signs of marquee activity. Then lurk. Obviously you will need to dress the part. Ask yourself, What would Fergie wear?

Swallow hard and copy.

If anyone stops you, just say, 'I'm with Giles,' and then laugh like a horse.

F OR THE BEST SNOGGING. School reunions: everyone regresses. It doesn't matter if you never went to the school; call yourself either Dave Thompson or Liz Smith and simply repeat, 'God, do you remember...?' every five minutes and let someone else finish off the memory.

FOR KNACKERED MUMS. If you're a mum who needs a bit of time to herself, then why not accidentally gate-crash your child into a local kids' party? If you're not sure where the nearest party is, just cruise around until you see some balloons on a door and lots of shifty-looking mums in a garden smoking and drinking dry white wine. OK, so your kid doesn't know any of the other kids, but once they've all had their faces painted, none of them recognise each other anyway. With any luck your child will receive a party bag containing enough cake and sweets to warrant cooking an evening meal unnecessary.

Similarly, if you take your children to a local activity centre – for example an ice rink or a bowling alley on a Saturday afternoon – you stand a good chance of shunting (a gentler form of crashing) them into a party. Look out for trestle tables set with party ephemera and nudge your kids into party pole position. Before they know it, they will be helping the birthday boy/girl blow out the candles and be stuffing themselves to the gunnels with cheap pizza. Well done, thinking mum.

CHIN UP GUIDE TO GATE-CRASHING

FOR THE BEST FRUIT CAKE

CHIN UP GUIDE TO GATE-CRASHING

FOR KNACKERED MUMS

FOR THE BEST FRUIT CAKE. Any funeral, really. Weirdly enough, this is also where you will find the randiest older women. Widows in black lace tend to get a bit saucy after a couple of sherries.

FOR THE BEST CELEBS. Elton John's White Tie and Tiara Ball is the biggest celeb party. Unless you're on first-name terms with Posh, prepare to polish up on your silver-service skills and apply to be a waitress. By the end of the night you could be in with a chance with one of the D-listers, or an A-lister who fancies a bit of rough.

CHIN UP GUIDE TO GATE-CRASHING

FOR MEN WHO ARE LOOKING FOR
THE BEST UP-FOR-IT WOMEN

work, they've all seen each other's breasts, and the novelty of mooning wore off about five hours ago. What they really want is a vaguely sober bloke who will pretend to listen and not get bored when they start crying. Tip: have some tissues and be prepared for them to vomit.

FOR STATIONERY. An office Christmas party. Just sneak into any old office block any day in December, follow the whiff of Britney Spears's latest perfume and within no time you'll be standing by a photocopier preparing to photocopy your genitals. Take the opportunity to raid any supplies of paper and ink before telling the boss to lick his own arse. Remember, he can't sack you: you don't work there. Make sure you have had your fill of cheese straws and sausage rolls before you pull this stunt.

FOR MEN WHO ARE LOOKING FOR THE BEST UP-FOR-IT WOMEN. Any hen party. There is something about a hen party that can bring out the slut in even the primmest Sunday-school teacher. It's that combination of excessive alcohol, stupid outfit and a tiny bit of jealousy about 'Mandy snaring a bloke' that can tip even 'nice' girls over the edge. All you need to do to crash a hen party is find one... Look in horrible big pubs, at Jongleurs comedy clubs and anywhere near a theatre that's been showing *The Vagina Monologues*. The closer to midnight, the easier it is to crash a hen party. They're meant to be women-only affairs, but beyond 9 p.m. the hens will have stopped caring. In fact, they're sick to the back teeth of each other, they've all got tinnitus from hearing each other shriek non-stop since they met up after

CHIN UP GUIDE TO GATE-CRASHING

FOR STATIONERY

Let's Slow Down

The trouble with progress is that it happens so fast that you don't have time to notice that things are disappearing before they've well and truly vanished off the face of the earth. Maybe if we just slowed down a bit, we'd remember to keep some of the things we're going to regret not having in the future.

50 THINGS WE'D BE BETTER OFF BRINGING BACK

(1) Fountain pens, inkwells, blotting paper and handwriting classes.

(2) Grammar – how to use a capital letter, the structure of a sentence and when to start a new paragraph.

(3) Chalk, blackboards and those blackboard rubbers that teachers can throw at kids who are behaving in a silly fashion at the back of the class.

(4) Lining up – if a teacher cannot make their class line up in a sensible and orderly fashion, then they should be instantly sacked.

(5) School assembly – there's nothing wrong with knowing a hymn or sitting cross-legged on the floor next to a pile of sick, which for some reason gets covered in sawdust, rather than simply cleaned away.

(6) Paper-boys (almost extinct in certain areas of London) – a child who has done a paper round all through a wet November is set up for life.

(7) Plaits – there is nothing to beat the excitement of pulling a girl's plait.

(8) French knitting – we didn't know why we did it, but it gave us something to do with our hands. It was the alternative to texting, and a lot more creative and colourful!

(9) Quilting – beat Cath Kidston at her own game. Really time-consuming and hard work, but what price an heirloom?

(10) Times tables done en masse in a sing-song voice.

(11) Learning things off by heart, rather than just Googling information when you need it. Once upon a time, every school kid knew at least one poem – this should be compulsory, and the compulsory poem should be *Hiawatha* by Henry Wadsworth Longfellow, which took the author eighteen months to write and takes about the same amount of time for children to learn.

(12) Cousins – they're good. Not as annoying as siblings. Cherish them; they make Christmases more interesting.

(13) Plain black wellington boots, please – we've had enough of all that 'Look at me; I'm so much fun; I've got zany wellies' nonsense.

(14) Proper light bulbs.

(15) Taps that have a blue blob on them for cold and a red blob on them for hot. Philippe Starck, my arse.

(16) Lesbian gym mistresses with sturdy legs in short pleated skirts – good news all round.

(17) Matrons with stiff hair and watches on their bosoms.

(18) White pepper – bound to come back in. Start using yours now.

(19) *Jackie* magazine – no wonder today's girls have lost their way. Bring back Cathy and Claire – every girl needs to know how to French-kiss with tongues but not be pressured into doing anything silly.

(20) Old women with hairnets and shopping baskets – forget all this trying to be young; let's hear it for women who are glad to be hideous old bags.

(21) Tin lids on Marmite jars. Plastic lids? No wonder the country's gone to the dogs.

(22) Proper party games like Sardines and Murder in the Dark, games that don't require plugs, batteries or charging up.

(23) Wooden tennis racquets.

(24) Cricket whites – what's all this coloured nylon nonsense? It's fine for the disco but not on the pitch.

(25) Darning – proper darning with a wooden mushroom.

(26) Egg cosies – felt ones are good. Children should learn to make these when they are nine.

(27)   *Top of the Pops* (on a Thursday night, thank you).

(28)   School custard in metal jugs – pink, lime and chocolate flavour to be liberally poured over spotted dick or a nice chocolate sponge.

(29)   Domestic-science lessons complete with baskets with plastic covers.

(30)   Cycling Proficiency badges.

(31)   The Tufty Club.

(32)   Stern children's TV presenters – no more pretending to be the kiddies' best friend; bring back the slightly austere/sadistic figure of authority.

(33)   Pen pals – it's always good to have someone to lie to about how exciting your life is.

(34)   Homemade rice pudding with skin on the top – the addition of a blob of jam is optional.

(35)   Diaries, not blogs – it's vital we don't lose the ability to write by hand.

(36)   Goitres and humpbacks – all the weird-looking ailments seem in danger of disappearing.

(37)   The Eleven-Plus and the non-fee-paying grammar school – the only fair way to sort out secondary education.

(38)   Nitty Nora the Hair Explorer.

(39)   Bath cubes – how very retro.

(40)   Learning how to do cross-stitch on that special material with the holes in it.

(41)   Handwritten thank-you letters – texts and emails do not count; notelets do. We demand a return.

(42)   Children's homemade birthday cakes that don't look like they've been anywhere near a professional cake decorator – bring back icing that's sliding off all over the place and those little silver balls that break your teeth.

(43)   Gabardine macs – smart and practical.

(44)   Satchels – how can you take pride in your schoolwork if you're carrying it around in a plastic bag?

(45)   Bowler hats for City gents – it's good to know who the bankers are.

(46)   Stamps in passports – preferably really fancy in peacock-green and purple ink.

(47) Looby Loo – without that weirdo Andy Pandy or those wet Flowerpot Men; this time round she'd be like a cross between Lady Gaga and Lily Allen.

(48) Soup spoons and their correct usage.

(49) Park attendants – really bad-tempered old blokes who were paid to shout at teenagers doing silly things in the park.

(50) The test card. Better than most Saturday-night telly. (Did you know that the original test-card girl was actually an eight-year-old Pam Ayres?)*

---

* This isn't actually true, but why not start a rumour? Remember, rumours are great and spreading them doesn't cost anything.

SOME OTHER RUMOURS YOU COULD SPREAD

Carla Bruni was once Samantha Cameron's pen pal.

Dove soap is called Dove because it contains a tiny amount of a sweet-smelling secretion that comes directly from a dove's anal glands.

Sebastian Coe had to have a sixth toe on his left foot amputated before finding success as an Olympic athlete.

Make up some more rumours and write them here:

_____

_____

_____

_____

Don't Bring Back

The trouble with nostalgia is that we tend to look back with rose-tinted specs, but here's a quick reminder that not everything was worth keeping. In fact, there are quite a few things from the past that really were truly awful and they include...

(1) Tapioca – or, as we called it, frogspawn, a dreadful dish that was more punishment than pudding.

(2) Smoking in confined spaces – smelly and cancerous.

(3) Asbestos. And lead paint for that matter.

(4) Half-day closing – do you remember the sheer tedium of half-day closing? In some small towns, a Wednesday afternoon was like something out of a really dismal fairy tale.

(5) Penny Farthings – an obviously stupid method of transport.

(6) *Encyclopaedia Britannica* – thank God for Google.

(7) *Stars on Sunday* – back in the 1970s, this was the only thing that was on TV on a Sunday evening – in some respects, this was a good thing, as the nation's children were so appalled by it that they would rather do their homework than suffer the strains of sanctimonious singing.

(8) Bri-nylon sheets – so full of static electricity you were in danger of setting the bed on fire, especially if you had unshaven, stubbly legs, as the friction between sheets and stubble could prove lethal.

(9) Old-fashioned sanitary towels – massive great bulky things that were attached by a safety pin to a weird plastic belt. Feminine hygiene at its worst, the old-fashioned sanitary towel was so complicated that it was only really fit for women with a degree in engineering.

(10) Hot pants – especially when worn with the above.

(11)   Prissy signs that said things like 'Tradesmen's entrance round the back.' People in the olden days could get away with being snobby and vile much more easily than we can now. It's good that old-fashioned class prejudice is on the way out, even if we do miss it sometimes.

(12)   Benny Hill.

(13)   Men-only golf clubs – once upon a time, women weren't welcome to join hundreds of golf clubs around the country. They're still not welcome, but there's nothing the old farts can do about it.

(14)   Hanging – even if we do bring back capital punishment, surely there are more modern ways of putting baddies down.

(15)   Dutch caps and spermicide.

(16)   The *Carry On* films – comebacks have already been attempted with disastrous results. Leave them alone.

(17)   Blancmange (and junket) – any pudding that requires rennet is bad.

(18)   Mr Blobby – he was an idiot.

(19)   Roland Rat – ditto. What was that all about? At least Pinky and Perky had style.

(20)   Noel Edmonds – oh God, we already brought him back. Why?

(21)   *Look and Learn*, an incredibly pompous educational magazine for children, who would inevitably rebel and want to take drugs as soon as one of these landed on the doormat.

(22)   Back-street abortions.

(23)   The Sinclair C5.

(24)   Minipops – weirdly sexually precocious six-year-olds who danced and sang on television for the delight of paedophiles all over the land. Really, their parents needed spaying for allowing them to be exploited in this fashion.

(25)   Re-usable condoms – yes, once upon a time condoms were big thick rubber things you could rinse out and use again. Nice!

(26)   Spittoons – receptacles for TB.

(27)   Cake eyeliner – a horrible dark brown 'cake' of compacted eyeliner that you had to spit on in order to moisten and hence turn into eyeliner that was liquid enough to run along your eyelids. As soon as the eyeliner was more than three days old, the spit would start

to react with the cake eyeliner and it would begin to smell. An indescribable smell that no other smell can emulate, it is the smell of stale spit on a cake of eyeliner.

(28) Telephone boxes – don't get sucked into the ridiculous notion that standing in a phone box was romantic. OK, so they looked like little red Tardises, but they were rubbish. You had to feed 2p pieces into slots that were all jammed up with chewing gum and the pips always went just when your boyfriend was going to tell you that he loved you. And obviously they smelled of wee, and some of them of poo!

(29) Press gangs – can you imagine it? There might be days when you want to get rid of your teenage son but you wouldn't want him press-ganged.

(30) Outside bathrooms – you can understand why people did poos in pots and put them under the bed.

(31) *On The Buses* – not funny.

(32) Betamax – never really took off in the first place.

(33) Manual typewriters – what a palaver! The ink ribbon (half red, half black – quite charming) would suddenly bulge and then get all tangled up and there was no way of putting the paper in straight. If you made a mistake, you had to use Tippex, which used to dry up and then you'd try and spit in it to make it work – what a mess.

(34) Gas at the dentist – can you imagine the horror? There you were, eleven years old, innocently going to the dentist, and the next thing you knew you were flat on your back with a massive rubber gas mask over your face and the dentist was counting, 'Ten, nine, eight... By the time I get to three, you will be...' Utterly petrifying. In fact, just thinking about it is upsetting me.

(35) *The Black and White Minstrel Show* – what were we thinking?

(36) Stockings and suspenders – it's a myth that these are sexy. The reality is very different, as any woman with a hefty thigh will tell you. There's nothing sexy about the tops of one's legs billowing over a pair of stockings like so much uncooked pizza dough.

(37) Slide rules – what a pointless waste of time they were. Hoorah for calculators and all that new-fangled 'cheating at maths'.

(38) No sex before marriage – hmmm, we think it's important to test the goods.

(39) Invalid carriages – as if the name wasn't bad enough.

(40) Complicated cameras with film – once upon a time, 99.9 per cent of the population didn't know how to use their cameras. Cameras were complicated, temperamental things, and if you accidentally opened the back, they would ruin your entire 36-picture reel of film. The other thing about old-fashioned complicated cameras was that you had no idea how hideous you looked until you'd paid for the film to be developed, whereupon you would break down in tears outside Boots. At least with digital cameras you can simply delete those photos that make you look like a cross between Arthur Mullard and a pig.

(41) Air raids – we've got enough to worry about without doodlebugs landing on our heads.

(42) Nouvelle Cuisine – oxymoronishly big in the 1980s. Overpriced, undersized food basically invented for people who were taking too much cocaine to ever get hungry.

(43) Roll-on girdles – underwear designed to control a woman's stomach and simultaneously squash her ovaries.

(44) Mangles – very dangerous. So easy to lose a breast in the mangle.

(45) Taking tonsils out on the kitchen table – a common occurrence, apparently. Really bad form, especially if the rest of the family were trying to eat.

(46) *Watch With Mother* – what if you hadn't got a mum? Back then, no one cared about that sort of thing. Obviously now things have gone too far the other way, but that's beside the point.

(47) Nail art – not to be confused with the rather common practice of decorating one's acrylic fingernails, nail art were dreadful pieces of so-called art that consisted of copper wire stretched across nails. These had been hammered into a board that had often been covered in purple velvet.

(48) The workhouse – thank goodness for benefits, eh?

(49) English coffee from before the American chains coming over and showing us how to do it. Dreadful stuff. We had no idea. English coffee was the pits. People only drank this hot brown water because it made them look sophisticated.

(50) Knitted swimming costumes – just silly.

Relationships
How Cost-Effective Are They?

It's important to weigh up the financial pros and cons of cohabiting. Is it enough to be in a relationship purely for companionship and a bit of sex? Yes, if both those things are of good quality, but for most people a relationship also needs to make sound economic sense. Cohabiting will often save money in the long term, as two people sharing the cost of a mortgage, electricity, gas, light bulbs, batteries for the remote control, dishwasher tablets, council tax and so on beats doing it on your tod.

However, there are other things to be taken into consideration. Joint payment of utility and household bills might be simple, but resentment can build up over petty little things, like the buying and using of toilet paper, biscuit consumption and going halves on petrol even when it's her parents that you're driving up to Inverness to see. So, before you move in together, here's a rough guide to...

The Financial Pros and Cons of Cohabiting (With a Woman)

Pros

- She will always have some cotton wool.
- You won't need to buy something from a shop if you need to go to a party dressed as a woman.

- She will have a stockpile of birthday cards that you can help yourself to in emergencies.

Cons

- She will scratch the car trying to get out of a multi-storey car park and make a great big mess of trying to cover up the scratch with nail varnish.
- She will spend a fortune on expensive low-calorie ready meals and then send you out for a Chinese when she's feeling peckish at 10 p.m.
- She will expect you to fix any little jobs that need doing round the house and if any of these jobs require a professional then you will have to pay for said professional as punishment for not being a professional yourself.

The Financial Pros and Cons of Cohabiting (With a Man)

Pros

- He can put you as a 'plus one' on his AA card.
- He's got a toolkit, so you don't have to waste your money on boring things like hammers and screwdrivers.
- Unlike living with another woman, he won't borrow your best dress and come back with a fag burn in it (unless he goes to a stupid fancy-dress party – see previous page).
- He won't nick your Slim Fast sachets or bunion pads, and you will save on buying razors because you can borrow his when your pits, legs and fanny need a tidy.

Cons

- He will never have a spare tampon when you need one. For this reason, it's worth thinking about lesbianism.
- He can go through a bottle of brown sauce in two days.
- He will tread on the mobile phone that you left charging on the floor (though that doesn't make it half your fault).
- He will slather your really expensive moisturiser on that nasty patch of eczema he's got under his armpit and that little tube of £45 Eve Lom spot cream on his haemorrhoids.
- If he's heavy, he will probably break the toilet seat.

Holidays for Two

One of the great advantages of being a couple is that you can share the cost of an early morning taxi to the airport. Enjoy this moment – you might not be speaking on the way back. Other benefits include:

For Her

➤ You won't have to pay a room supplement for having a double room all to yourself – not unless he snores so much you need to book a separate suite.

➤ You can use up what's left of your sun tan lotion on his big fat back rather than risk bringing it home in your suitcase and it leaking all over your summer wardrobe.

➤ You won't have to fight off young men in tiny swimming trunks who pretend to love you but basically want to con you out of your life savings.

For Him

➤ You will have someone to go drinking with of an evening, rather than bankrupting yourself by draining the mini bar because you're too embarrassed to be seen knocking back gin and tonics by yourself in the hotel bar.

➤ She will probably have some sort of cream that will help when you burn the top of your bald pate and you are peeling so badly that you are secretly frightened that eventually you will peel so much that your brain will be exposed.

➤ Thanks to her ability to cry at the drop of a hat, you've got a much better chance of getting a room upgrade – nine times out of ten hysterics work better than calm reasoning – they will want her out of that foyer asap.

Cooking for Two

Cooking for two is just as easy as cooking for one. However, it can be more expensive, so try not to pick a really greedy one. It's also good to get one who doesn't mind cheap things like beans on toast... or just toast.

WEDDINGS

ARE THEY WORTH IT?

Let's just say you've successfully cohabited for a while. Maybe you've survived your first dreadful holiday together, seen each other be sick/have diarrhoea and been introduced to each other's freakish friends and family. For many couples, the next logical step is marriage, but let's just pause for a second – are weddings worth it?

Um… no. Thing is, you can't get your money back if the marriage turns out to be faulty or breaks down altogether.

A wedding is the single most expensive thing you are ever going to fork out for that comes with absolutely no money-back guarantee.

Obviously you can claw back some cash by flogging the rings and the dress, but the marquee hire, the catering, DJ, fireworks, those ridiculous little bags of sugared almonds for the guests – when it all goes tits up, it's just money down the drain.

So, before you get married, stop and ask yourself, percentage-wise, how convinced you are that this is going to work.

100 per cent convinced

Go for it. Hire that Scottish castle, demand those bagpipes, cover everything with Swarovski crystals, get Anton du Beke to choreograph the first dance. Personally, I give it two years.

80–99 per cent convinced

You're taking a gamble, but it's your choice. There's a nagging 'what if?' at the back of your mind, but it's probably too late to cancel, and anyway, you really fancy the Maldives for your honeymoon, so you might as well go for the six bridesmaids, the running buffet and the disco after. Don't blame me if you start hating his guts halfway over the Indian Ocean.

60–80 per cent convinced

Sensible girl. It's worth a punt, but don't go mad – go for the mid-range package: the local church, marquee in a relative's back garden, honeymoon in France. Who knows – with any luck you might have backed yourself a winner.

40–60 per cent convinced

Well, you've got your doubts. Best to err on the side of caution: keep it small, a nice registry do with a really great hat and a handful of people for lunch in the pub.

20-40 per cent convinced

Are you sure you want to bother? Hmm, why not stick to being 'engaged'? Considering you've already slept with his brother, you'd be better off saving your money and keeping your options open.

0-20 per cent convinced

Why not just go and put 25 grand on the dogs?

Divorce: Is It Worth the Hassle and Expense?

No, which is why you should have a really serious think before you get married. Divorce is very simple; basically, you both end up with half as much as you had when you were still together. However, thanks to the advent of the iPlayer, at least separating the record collection isn't half the trauma that it used to be.

Before You Tie the Knot... Let's Just Think About Those Vows

For better, for worse

If he trips up and breaks his leg as you're leaving the church, it's a bad sign: leave him before the ink is dry on the marriage certificate; he's only going to drag you down.

For richer, for poorer

There is no point not being better off than you were as a singleton; this is surely the first rule of marriage. A decent husband or wife should be able to save you money in the long run.

What **he** should be able to do to save you money

- Assemble flat-pack furniture.
- Charge a car battery.
- Climb a ladder without getting silly and faint.
- Drive long distances without getting weepy.
- Be assertive on holiday so that you don't get ripped off.
- Give you a piggyback home so that you don't have to get a cab. (You can't walk because you are wearing silly heels.)

What **she** should be able to do to save you money

- Listen, so that you don't end up needing professional counselling.
- Help you choose your clothes so that you don't make expensive mistakes that you're too embarrassed to return to the shops.
- Buy you nice birthday presents so you don't end up spending your own money on that leather Paul Smith iPhone cover.
- Make meals that are nearly as tasty as ones in fancy restaurants but not quite, so that going out for a meal is still a nice treat.
- Make shoes last.
- Watch *The Wire* on telly so that you don't have to fork out for the box set.

In sickness and in health

Get a nice robust partner – look out for the ones that are well covered in fat (but not too well covered) and have a nice healthy glow (but do not confuse a nice healthy glow with someone who has been drinking at lunchtime). Sickly ones tend to cost a fortune in cold and flu relief and have ongoing ailments like verrucas and athlete's foot, which can not only be contagious but are expensive to treat.

Till death us do part

Or divorce, which I have already told you is really expensive and makes you feel completely cheated and conned. Unfortunately divorce is sometimes inevitable. This can happen for many reasons. You don't fancy him. He doesn't fancy you. He fancies your mate Hilary. He's slept with your mate Hilary (she's now known as 'that whore Hilary').

RENT-A-WIFE

Bored and lonely? Missing that special someone in your life? Then look no further. For just fifteen quid an hour, rent yourself a wife.

Rent-a-Wife will come round to your house, complain about the state of the place, nag you into doing some DIY, refuse to have sex and then huff off back to her mother's. Guaranteed to cause an argument within the first five minutes, **Rent-a-Wife** is a cheap and easy reminder of why being single isn't so bad after all.

OR:

For just another £4.99, why not choose the **Adoring Her Indoors**? Guaranteed to stand by the window for hours on end just waiting for you to come home.

OR, FOR THE SAME PRICE:
The Good Plain Cook
pig ugly but makes great gravy.

OR HOW ABOUT:
The Filthy Slut
can't cook, but wears suspenders.

RENT-A-HUSBAND

Bored and lonely? Missing that special someone in your life? Then look no further. For just fifteen quid an hour, rent yourself a husband.

Rent-a-Husband will come round to your house, disappear behind a newspaper, promise to do something about that damp patch in the spare room, then bugger off down the pub.

Introducing

THE FAIR-SHARES
REMOTE CONTROL

- Comes with an automatic timer
- Senses when HE has been hogging too much testosterone telly and automatically searches for a BONNET DRAMA or a SOAP to balance the evening's viewing

TO MAKE A MARRIAGE WORK

You (the woman) will have to be patient and he (the man) will have to make sure he's not an idiot. Marrying an idiot is one of the silliest things a woman can do. The trouble is, over the past few years women have turned into bitches and men have turned into ninnies. It's probably time women tried to be nicer and men tried not to be so wet.

Men, this country needs you... to be men.

Obviously we still want you to be sensitive, period-pain aware and capable of making a really good fish pie, but we'd also like you to relearn some *man* skills. In fact, from now on no man will be allowed to get married until he has proved himself DIY adequate. He shall remain a bachelor, living with his mother, until he's passed a Little Jobs Around the House course. This would cover such basics as bleeding a radiator and removing a dead pigeon from the gutter (without gagging).

Women, on the other hand, would be allowed to retain their domestic martyr status and to keep the secret of the washing machine. For some reason, it's an unwritten law that women should be permitted to pretend that there's some big mystique about putting a wash on and that operating the tumbler-dryer is a bit trickier than splitting the atom. They only do this because they don't want men to know it's a piece of piss.

Other domestic lies that women tell include the 'I'm busy in the kitchen' fib. Translation: 'I'm busy reading *Take a Break* magazine, swigging sherry from the bottle and eating a family-sized cheesecake with my hands.' And of course the biggest domestic lie of all: 'I've got a headache.'

Men and women should start

respecting each other again. Men are going to come to terms with the fact that women are lazy, self-obsessed, sentimental old windbags who don't like putting petrol in the car (not with our money, anyway). Whereas women are going to have to come to terms with the fact that men are great big hairy bags of wobbling insecurity who need constant affection, approval, brown sauce and blow-jobs.

Men and women can be quite good together, especially when they have kids in common and need to present a united front. Children actually don't want their parents to get divorced. It can affect them badly – for example, a friend of mine started wetting the bed when his parents split up; this led in turn to difficulties within his own marriage, as he was 34 at the time and his wife got fed up with sharing a bed with a leaky neurotic.

Tolerance – that's the key to bringing down divorce rates.

WOMEN ARE GOING TO HAVE TO UNDERSTAND

- His idiot single friend who smells.
- The fact he puts brown sauce on everything, including salmon.
- You can't share books on holiday, because his are weird.
- He doesn't like making phone calls.
- The supermarket frightens him.
- He prefers his mother's shepherd's pie (possibly because it contains a lot of brown sauce).
- He can't stand musicals/reality TV/*Loose Women*.
- You must not talk during *Top Gear*.

MEN ARE GOING TO HAVE TO UNDERSTAND

- The fact that sometimes crying does her good.
- She likes *Cranford*, and crying at *Cranford* is one of her biggest pleasures in life.
- She would be really upset if a burglar came in and stole that silver box the children's baby teeth are in – not because the box is valuable but because the teeth are invaluable.
- A muddy floor really isn't a laughing matter.

Do you Really WANT KIDS?

Think long and hard about whether you really want children in the first place. Children are greedy and silly. So, why have them? Answer: you might need a kidney one day.

If you haven't already started a family then hold your horses

A child costs on average £200,000 to raise. Just think of all the things you could buy with £200,000

A list of things you could have:

(1) Loads of really nice clothes
(2) A car and a caravan or some racehorses
(3) Your hair properly cut and coloured every six months for the rest of your life
(4) A personal trainer or the equivalent in liposuction
(5) Seventy designer handbags
(6) Your own set of skis and a ski holiday once a year (till you get sick of breaking a limb every time you go on a stupid skiing holiday).

Think shoes? Or babysitters? Shoes? Or babysitters.

Weigh up the Pros and Cons

PRO   Getting pregnant will give you an excuse to feel special and eat biscuits.

CON   It will make you fat, with a special indelible fat that never really comes off.

PRO   Having a child means you will have someone to look after you in your old age. Hoorah – you put up with them sticking your shoes down the toilet and scribbling on the walls, now it's their turn to put up with you weeing on the sofa and hiding the remote control down your knickers.

CON   They might just put you into a really cheap place where they tie you to a commode for 24 hours a day. Ha! It's payback for that potty training.

PRO   Babies are sweet, they love you and think you are clever.

CON   This doesn't last: by the time your child is about ten, they will have started to suspect you are an idiot; by the time they are a teenager, they will think you are stupider than a piece of stupid shit on the end of a stupid stick that was left in the stupid park.

PRO   Babies grow into toddlers who are quite funny and come into your bed for snuggles.

CON   They only come into your bed because they have pissed their own bed. Try pissing the bed yourself and see whether they're so keen to get in.

If you Decide to Embark on Family Life

Ⓐ Breastfeed: it doesn't cost anything and you don't have to sterilise your nipples (not unless you've gone and got them really dirty – say they've got soil on them). Unfortunately you can't breastfeed children forever. It's no good trying to save on school dinners by feeding them through the railings.

Ⓐ Try to time it so that you have your children a year after all your friends have had theirs: this means you will get all the cast-offs. Leave it much longer and they will start re-breeding and keeping stuff in bin liners for 'the new baby'.

Ⓐ Try to see your child not just as an exhausting drain on your purse and your emotions but as a positive thing. For example, now you've had a baby you've got an excuse to have post-natal depression and lie on the sofa eating cheap biscuits. Obviously this isn't funny if you really are depressed, but it's worth trying it on for a couple of days.

Ⓐ This is your chance to get your man (if he's still around) to do stuff. All you need to say to make him hop to attention is, 'Crikey, I think I might have just popped a stitch.' He will be so scared of some more blood and poo falling out of your bottoms (front and back) that he will scurry around picking stuff up for you for months. Remember men have 'birth flashbacks'; apparently these can be worse than fighting the Vietcong.

Check out your Kiddie-Compatibility Rating

It's probably best you don't have a baby if...

- 🐣 You mind jam being smeared all over your plasma telly.
- 🐣 You find it hard to shift weight – you won't.
- 🐣 You truly believe that you and only you are the centre of the universe.
- 🐣 You're not sure you could trust your husband not to drop it.
- 🐣 You get easily bored by things.
- 🐣 The sight of poo or snot makes sick come up into your mouth – mind you, if you can't beat them, why not join them? Babies are forever puking up. See how they like having vomit in *their* hair.
- 🐣 You like a lie-in of a morning.
- 🐣 You have a low pain threshold. It's not just the getting them out of your fanny that smarts a bit, it's all the other things: trapping your fingers in the collapsing buggy, treading on Lego with bare feet, falling over stupid toys on the stairs. Plus babies do that really annoying thing of gouging your face and pulling your hair, and you're not even allowed to do it back.
- 🐣 You like going out and getting drunk and maybe not coming home for a couple of days.
- 🐣 You've got more than four dogs.
- 🐣 You are living on a mate's sofa.
- 🐣 You've just bought a really expensive pair of jeans that only fit if you don't have lunch – wait till you've let yourself go and then think about it.
- 🐣 The idea of stretch marks makes you want to kill yourself.
- 🐣 You're meant to be doing your GCSEs in nine months' time.
- 🐣 You like pulling wings off flies.

ASK NOT WHAT YOU CAN DO FOR YOUR CHILDREN BUT **WHAT THEY CAN DO FOR YOU**

WHAT CAN THEY DO?

Now that sweeping chimneys is no longer legal, we need to think long and hard about how children can be a financial asset to their parents and not just a great big money-sucking leech.

ARE THEY ATTRACTIVE?

If your child is attractive, they could model. Now, before you get excited, ask yourself whether you or your partner is remotely good-looking. If the answer to that is 'No, not really', then the chances are, your child will not be model material. Oh well, better luck next time. Maybe if you swap partners, you might get a nicer-looking kid.

OK, let's just imagine for a moment that your child is agreeable to look at. What sort of look has your child got? If they look like they just fell out of an Enid Blyton book and don't mind wearing round-toed shoes and Fair Isle sweaters, then they can do Boden and the White Company catalogues. Note: it helps here if you have given your child a Victorian servant's name, like Molly or Stan. Also, do not give your child a Nike shaved hairdo if this is the kind of work you are aiming for.

If you've accidentally given your child a common name and they look a bit like something you'd see hanging off a pram in Lidl, then you might have a chance with frozen-food advertising or Sun Holidays. If your child looks like a malnourished little match-seller, don't despair – they might be just what the NSPCC are looking for for their Christmas campaign.

ARE THEY PRECOCIOUS?

Could your child be a prodigy? This is more likely if both parents are quite bright. (For example, if Mum and Dad both have very high, boffin-style foreheads, then the kid might be in with a chance of being a genius.) Unfortunately, most parents think their kid is a genius, when in fact they are boringly average.

However, on the off-chance that you might have delivered a gifted child, it's probably best to give them a clever-sounding name. Any of the following will do: Corinthian, Isolde, Pythagoras and Ganymede.

WARNING
If by the time they are in primary school they still can't spell their own name, chances are you've bred a dud.

Let's just say your child has prodigy potential; now you've got to decide what sort of prodigy you want them to be. Traditionally, you've got a choice between music, ballet/ice-skating and chess. All these things will involve travelling the world and staying in nice hotels, so if you fancy this kind of lifestyle, it's best to start pushing your child as early as possible. You can make their lives simpler by choosing them a musical instrument that hardly any other kid plays. This will make it easier for them to be 'the best in the world'. Most musical prodigies are given violins. Why not give yours a zither or a balalaika? Ditto board games – bright children are pushed into playing chess, so why not make yours unbeatable at something like Buckaroo or Operation?

Basically, whatever the kid is good at, make sure they are really good at it by the age of nine. This is the cut-off age for being a child prodigy. The trouble with being a child prodigy is that a lot of them peak at about twelve and then don't do much except struggle to live in the shadow of their own past. Try to make some decent money out of them before this happens.

If your kid is precocious without being especially talented, get them to write a book. Remember, kids under ten are a billion times more likely to be published than a woman in her late 40s.

AND REMEMBER, IF ALL ELSE FAILS, PUT THEM ON EBAY.

Kids in these Belt-Tightening Days

Kids these days expect too much; they're spoiled and it's got to stop. From now on it should be illegal for a child to have their own TV set in their bedroom. As for being given a choice at mealtimes? We never were, and apart from developing a lifelong phobia about liver and crying if I ever see rice pudding with a skin on it, it's never done me any harm.

What children need to learn is that life is tough and semolina is horrible, but at least you should try it. They don't need mobile phones and ridiculous trainers with flashing lights. Parents, it's up to you to just say no (and mean it).

LOWERING THEIR EXPECTATIONS

Kids too can do their bit during these difficult days and they can begin by generally lowering their expectations. For starters, they can have birthday parties like we had birthday parties. None of this party-bag nonsense: they can have a balloon, a piece of cake and then they can fuck off home.

If you really feel pressurised into the party-bag nonsense, get down to your local pound shop, pick up a load of things for a quid, then wrap them up in newspaper and make a lucky dip. The fact that none of the gifts is going to be that 'lucky' will be a valuable life lesson – sometimes what you get is a bit rubbish, especially when you are ten and your lucky gift turns out to be some peculiar butterscotch wafer biscuits, a tin of shoe polish or a packet of confetti. Tough.

START BY EXPLODING THE MYTH OF THE TOOTH FAIRY

Kids these days expect a quid a tooth; some get £2. Obviously this is madness. We need to tell our children, 'There is no Tooth Fairy. Your tooth fell out because baby teeth look stupid in an adult's great big face. Grow up. There is no Tooth Fairy.'

Kids have 20 milk teeth. That's 20 quid saved per kid. Therefore if you have three children, you could save yourself 60 quid. Quick – go out and buy yourself ten bottles of decent wine.

If your children insist that there is a Tooth Fairy, say, 'OK, but the Tooth Fairy is a vengeful fairy, and if the tooth is heavy with plaque or there's a hint of filling, then she's not going to pay up.' In fact, tell them that the Tooth Fairy is quite capable of charging for the collection of poor-quality teeth and if your brats aren't careful they might get a bill from the Tooth Fairy, who is sick to death of having to cart away stinking, rotten teeth in the middle of the night. This could be anything from 50p to £3. Just think – if your child has particularly bad teeth, you could collect £60 in tooth fines. Times this by three children and, hey presto, you've made yourself £180 – you know it makes sense. Now you can afford those boots you have your eye on in Hobbs.

TOYS

Children don't need all these toys. If they've got an imagination, they will be happy with a cardboard box.

THINGS YOU CAN PRETEND A CARDBOARD BOX IS

- a doll's house
- a racing car
- a cardboard box full of imaginary puppies. Ah, what shall we call the puppies?

But what do you do if your child isn't happy with a cardboard box (and can't think what to call the imaginary puppies). Once you've come to terms with the fact that your child has zero imagination, then it's time for Plan B. Now that you know they aren't going to be arty, try to encourage them to be proficient at accountancy – basically, all this type of kid needs is sums.

KIDS, ARE YOU TOO SKINT TO GO OUT AND HAVE FUN WITH YOUR MATES? THEN WHY NOT STAY AT HOME AND SULK?

Yes, sulking is a great way to waste your time without spending any money. It's also a great way to drive your mum and dad *mad* if you've gone and had your Xbox confiscated and they've taken away your hand-held games console. That's right – you just need to spend hours on your bed with a massive great donkey on your lip, hating everything and everybody.

Just fold your arms, curve your spine and force the corners of your mouth to turn down – practise in a mirror and you'll soon get the hang of it. Ah, the joy of sulking.

MOTHERS

send them somewhere really dull out of London with no mobile signal.

They'll come home and appreciate you.

CORRECTIVE TROUSER TRAINING

FOR YOUNG MEN WHO HAVE LOST THE ABILITY TO PULL THEIR JEANS ABOVE THEIR BUM-LINES

THE TROUBLE WITH HOLIDAYS

Another great bonus of a faltering economy is that we now have an excuse not to go on holiday. Phew – that's this year's summer sorted out. Holidays are horribly hard work, unless you are lithe and sporty and look good on a beach, in which case you probably aren't English. For most of us, our summer holidays are spent resenting our nearest and dearest and wishing we weren't so fat.

The trouble with holidays is that there is such a gulf between what we want and what we get. Middle-aged women always think they're going to find some fantastic leather shoes in a tucked-away market square. The reality is being stung by a jellyfish and a stranger insisting on pissing on the sting in full view of a gawping crowd.

Unfortunately, the notion that we all need a holiday is so wired into the British psyche that even when times are hard, it's impossible to let it go, which is why some of us end up going camping.

CAMPING

On a sliding scale of holidays, camping in Britain is at the bottom. The only way camping could get any worse would be if you had to share a tent with Mr Methane – a man who farts for a living.

Camping is only acceptable if it's a dad taking his kids away for a bonding weekend of campfires and burnt sausages. There is no need to involve the mother; she could maybe stay in a nearby boutique hotel and visit for a couple of hours in the afternoon, if the weather's nice.

Camping abroad is only acceptable if you go to one of those campsites where they put the tent up for you and your accommodation includes separate sleeping compartments, a fully stocked fridge and a nice bit of wooden decking complete with a gas-fired barbecue. Oh, and a really fit French dad camping next door in a pair of teeny trunks that you can have appallingly filthy dreams about, leading to complaints from other campers about the noises you make while you are masturbating.

A step up from camping is caravanning. The only thing you need to remember when you are caravanning is to take a lot of vodka and some playing cards, because this is what you will spend your holiday doing – drinking vodka and playing poker while it rains.

 Make sure you don't drink all the vodka on the first night; you will need some for splashing on your cornflakes when you wake up in the morning and it's still pissing down.

STAYING IN A B&B

The next step up from caravanning is staying in a B&B somewhere 'cheap and cheerful' by the sea. The phrase 'cheap and cheerful' is an oxymoron; the two things cannot coexist and the phrase should be reinvented as 'cheap and a bit depressing'. However, some of us don't have a choice, so…

Try and turn it into an adventure. Pretend that staying in a rubbish B&B in Fleetwood is 'ironic'. Or pretend you are in a gritty kitchen-sink-style film and that you are playing a character who is poor at the moment but is just about to become rich and successful. Or smuggle in some booze; if you have booze and a telly, then everything's OK, especially once you've drunk quite a lot of booze.

Wherever you stay make sure you ask the receptionist, 'Are the sheets Indian cotton?' Doesn't matter what the response is; just those words coming out of your mouth will make you feel as rich as royalty, or at least as rich as Laurence Llewelyn-Bowen.

Another sure-fire way to get preferential treatment in some crappy B&B is to follow this simple rule: when you're booking the room and they ask for your name, reply, 'Lady Winthrop, but just call me Elaine.' With any luck this will upgrade you to a room without mouse droppings.

HIRING A HOLIDAY COTTAGE

Going self-catering might save you loads of money but doesn't really constitute a holiday considering that you end up doing exactly the same as you do at home but with different pots and pans! Great.

Instead, go and stay with an old school friend. Ha! That will teach her for bullying you. Who's having the last laugh? You are – sitting in her conservatory, drinking her sherry. How the tables have turned... bitch!

VOLUNTEERING HOLIDAYS

There are lots of ways of getting accommodation cheaply if, for example, you're prepared to chip your nail varnish building a dry-stone wall in the Lake District in the middle of winter.

WARNING
They will probably expect you to wear an Aran jumper as well as chip your nail varnish. Some holidays just aren't worth the hassle.

IF IT'S ALL TOO MUCH TO BEAR, WHY NOT... STAY AT HOME?!

Save money on an exotic holiday: don't go anywhere. Simply sit in a deck chair in your front room, pop the electric fire on, close your eyes and you could be in the Caribbean. The trick is not to open your eyes for a fortnight... Easy.

A Simple Lesson in Maths
The Rule of Kids and Holidays

The problem with holidays if you're a parent is that you have to pay for the children, and once they're over two and you're no longer breastfeeding, this can get a tad pricey. Basically:

FEWER KIDS MEAN BETTER HOLIDAYS.

This is a simple mathematical equation. Holidays divided by children creates a sliding scale: the more children you have, the less likely you are to have a nice holiday somewhere decent. So, if you want a nice holiday in a pleasant hotel, then make sure you don't have more than two children.

One Child

With one child, you can have Barbados at Christmas, a fortnight in Italy in the summer and as many child-free city breaks as you like, because the grandparents can cope with one kid. The trouble with all these romantic city breaks is that as your alcohol units rocket, so does your libido and you will accidentally find yourself up the duff again. Say goodbye to exotic holidays. Nana and Grandpa can cope with one, but two might give Grandpa a stroke.

Some parents might think even two children is going to make holidays a bit too expensive and decide to only have one, preferably a small one who can sleep on a heap of towels at the foot of their hotel bed. This is actually false economy, as the child will be so bored and lonely without a sibling to bicker with that you will spend most of your holiday in a local toy shop bribing them with expensive crap that will allow you to lie on the beach for ten minutes before they start whining again.

Two Children

Wales at Easter with another couple who have children the same age. This will be a disaster because you will have completely opposing ideas about childrearing and you won't be able to stand the way their kids are so spoiled and ungrateful. They, in turn, will think yours are prissy and boring (or vice versa – there are endless permutations around this scenario).

Summer: a Mark Warner in Portugal. It will cost a bomb, but anything to get the kids off your back. Unfortunately, your two will refuse to go to the kids' club, preferring instead to bicker with each other, get upset tummies and cry because they don't like the 'lovely sand'. The weather will also be a bit disappointing.

Three Children

A trip to a museum at half-term and a week in a bungalow in Cornwall during the summer. All this will be a blur of lost nooo-nooos, trying to find a toilet, teething rings and dirty nappies in your handbag because there aren't any bins any more.

Your marriage is officially on the at-risk register.

Four Children

A planned day out to Brighton during the Easter holidays, which will be cancelled due to rain, and a summer break in the Sherwood Forest Center Parcs (with any luck one or two of them might get lost in the woods). To save money, you will have booked a smaller chalet than you actually need. This results in sharing a bed with your three-year-old, who for some reason turns into a bag of wee at night.

Remember:

FOUR KIDS OR MORE = AN EXPENSIVE CAR.

FIVE CHILDREN

If you have five children, there is a chance you are very posh and very rich, in which case you (plus nannies) will bunk off for weeks at a time to various estates in Scotland and Jamaica. If, however, you are not rich, you will spend four days camping in Norfolk. It would have been a week, but you'd rather put a tent peg through your face than stay another day.

Go Away When It's Not Holiday Time

That is to say when the kids have gone back to school, including yours. Ha! That will teach them, the whining ingrates. Serves them right if they're slaving away doing really boring stuff like physics and double maths while you and the old man are whooping it up on the Costa (not as much without them) Smeralda.

OTHER HOLIDAY EXPENSES THAT YOU ARE LIKELY TO INCUR IF YOU HAVE A LARGE BROOD

It's not just the cost of the ice creams, snorkels and flippers that's going to interfere with your sangria budget; once you have three or more children, you can't go anywhere without getting more than one cab. Legally, you will have to get two, unless you've got a driver who doesn't mind if one of your brats sits on your knee without a seat belt. After all, it's not his problem if little Michaela goes through the windscreen; he's not going to have to sit opposite her scarred face at the breakfast table every day.

WHAT CHILDREN
DO NOT NEED ON HOLIDAY

- more than one ice cream a day
- a lilo in the shape of something just because some other kid has got one
- a deep-sea diving watch
- electronic games that make stupid noises on the beach – what's wrong with a book?!*
- a castle-shaped bucket (cheating)

They also do not need to go to Disneyland – it's not a right. Put them off the idea by telling them the cartoon characters are kept in cages and treated worse than battery chickens. Which is probably true. In fact, given a choice, I would rather be a battery chicken, eating my own faeces and pecking at my own skin, than be a cartoon character at Disneyland. Kids don't really appreciate spectacle. I took my daughter to a zoo once and her favourite animal was an orange plastic litter bin in the shape of a squirrel.

HINT

If your child bangs on about Disneyland until you are both blue in the face, then pretend to take them to Disneyland Paris – go to a small local theme park or funfair and tell them it's Disneyland. Disorient them by waking them very early in the morning and letting them see that you have passports. Then put them in the car and drive for seven hours in a very big circle. With any luck they will be so disorientated by the time that you get to 'Disneyland Paris' they will be too overexcited to notice the difference. Remember to make a big fuss about needing euros for the car park and for extra authenticity pack some croissants.

---

* Pah! In my day...

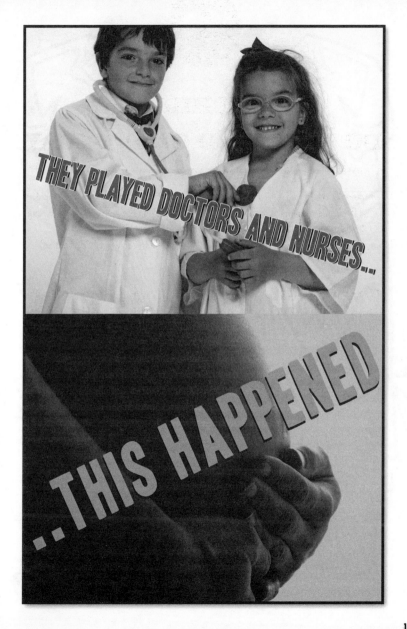

Bring
Back
the
Battleaxe

Our streets are awash with sick and spit, yobs urinate in full view (and that's just the girls), and good, upstanding people are too afraid to do anything about it. The time has come to wheel out our weapon of mass destruction. Not community policemen with silly fluorescent waistcoats, not tear gas or ASBOs. No, what this country needs is to bring back the battleaxe.

Once upon a time, the battleaxe was everywhere. These were women whose invisibility had mutated into unavoidability, women whose sheer girth and bossiness meant that they stopped any nonsense or bad behaviour in its tracks. Corseted in waist-length bras, bulky tweed coats (whatever the weather) and black lace-up shoes, they were effectively bossiness in a bulletproof body protector.

Your classic battleaxe could iron a shirt in two swift movements, had 50 uses for bicarb and didn't sit down till everything was done. Trained to sniff out silliness and shoddiness, she could plonk herself in the middle of a disturbance, stand her ground and scare the shit out of everyone.

....

Be Proud to Be a Battleaxe

Rather than all of us fighting invisibility and seeing it as the scourge of the middle-aged woman, we need to work with it. Instead of desperately trying to redress the balance by wearing attention-seeking clothes, plunging necklines and spending all our time at the gym, we urge older women everywhere to embrace their invisibility, throw away their

How to Get Into the Battleaxe Zone

Here are some things you might like to say to get you in the mood... You will have to accompany these with tuts and shaking of the head.

☙

Have you seen the state of her washing?

☙

I wouldn't give it houseroom.

☙

That cake is shop-bought.

☙

She's all fur and no knickers.

☙

You mark my words.

☙

That child wants slapping.

☙

You must think I was born yesterday.

(Er... no, actually.)

Good Battleaxe Names

/⚡

Bessie

/⚡

Betty

/⚡

Beryl

/⚡

Myrtle

/⚡

Gladys

/⚡

Alma

/⚡

Elsie

hair-straighteners, HRT patches and sling-backs and buy a big hairnet, a wicker basket (to snag the legs of people in queues) and a stick (to wave menacingly at people).

Ladies, let's explore our inner battleaxe. We can let our moustaches grow, wrap our varicose veins up in big, thick support stockings and 'tell it like it is'. Becoming a battleaxe means we can develop a lardy-cake habit, wear horrible hats and rule the roost at home. No one will mess with us. People will stand up and offer us seats on buses and trains, not out of respect but out of sheer fear. Cap-doffing will come back!

We'll make battleaxing fashionable. Women will be queuing round the block for battleaxe make-overs – buying products to encourage whiskery chins and clamouring for vintage National Health bottle-lens glasses. We need to commandeer Boys' Brigade halls and turn them into battleaxe training centres, complete with lots of whistleblowing and a plentiful supply of TCP.

How to Spot a Battleaxe

A woman who:

Cooks and never uses a recipe book.

/⚡

Knows the difference between a soft and a hard broom.

/⚡

Boils her net curtains in bleach or bicarbonate of soda.

/⚡

Bathes in bicarb.

/⚡

Uses starch in her ironing.

Knows how to get a bad stain
out of a cotton shirt.

🪓

Runs a neat airing cupboard.

🪓

Has a nose that can detect bacteria
at a sniff, thereby making
sell-by dates redundant.

🪓

Can sniff out soup that
has seen a packet.

🪓

Can run rings round gormless
shop assistants and make
them cry or get them the sack.

🪓

Holds her handbag out
for buses to stop.

🪓

Instils the fear of God
into youths.

🪓

Can do mental arithmetic and
confuse shop assistants who can't.

🪓

Knows when she is handed under-
weight helpings of ham.

🪓

Knows what to do with
offal and tripe.

🪓

Likes a pair of slippers she
can peg out washing in.

🪓

Refuses to cast a clout
till May is out.

Famous Battleaxes

🪓 **Boadicea**
killer battleaxe

🪓 **Queen Victoria**
battleaxe in a
bonnet who was
never amused

🪓 **Grandma
from the Giles
cartoons**
scary battleaxe

🪓 **Margaret
Thatcher**
despot battleaxe

🪓 **Barbara
Woodhouse**
battleaxe with a
dog

🪓 **Barbara
Cartland**
battleaxe in pink

🪓 **Ena Sharples**
soap battleaxe

🪓 **Fanny Cradock**
kitchen battleaxe

🪓 **Nora Batty**
the battleaxe who
gave stockings a
bad name – good!

🪓 **The Queen**
royal battleaxe

🪓 **Ann
Widdecombe**
virgin battleaxe

Pull Yourselves Together
or Reasons to Be Cheerful

Suddenly everyone is having an emotional journey or having to find 'closure', which is putting a terrible strain on valuable NHS resources as a great deal of time and energy is wasted on soppy therapies of one sort or another.

We are not saying that the clinically depressed, the sad and confused shouldn't be treated with absolute kindness, care and consideration; we're just saying that there are time-wasters out there who are directing sympathy away from more well-deserving causes. Basically, not everyone is suffering from a medical condition; some people are just behaving like selfish twats.

A perfect case in point is the sudden popularity among C-list celebrities of blaming everything – from snorting cocaine to dressing their children like chavs – on being bi-polar. Pah! In my day, being bi-polar meant that you'd walked to both Poles, not that you enjoyed lolling around in your dressing gown all day waiting for a delivery of class-A drugs. Another celebrity syndrome is sex addiction, which is just an excuse for sportsmen who can't keep it in their trousers.

We need to stem this tide of nonsense. So here are some simple remedies or self-help alternatives that cost nothing and are demonstrably just as effective as going to see a shrink or taking mood-changing drugs.

Feeling Generally Low?

Build a bonfire. Set aside a crisp, windy autumn day, put up a deck chair, bake a potato and make a day of it. Watch the embers and some falling leaves, feel good about getting rid of a load of old crap that has been cluttering up the shed and come back in smelling of wood smoke, with your cheeks all lovely and rosy and your eyes all bright – better than a fancy day at a spa.

Try whistling. Whistling is the easiest way to fake cheerfulness. You can be feeling completely suicidal, but as long as you are whistling something jolly, no one would ever guess. Hopefully, if you whistle long enough and hard enough, you might even be able to con yourself that everything's OK. There – how much did that cost? Nothing.*

Bored and Listless?

Try bird-watching. Buy a really good pair of binoculars, a bird-spotting book, a bird table and some nuts, then sit back and wait for Mother Nature's bird-table extravaganza. When you get fed up with waiting for a little yellowhammer to land on your bird table and you've eaten all the nuts, you might want to use the binoculars for something else – like looking at your neighbour's washing or prying into other people's bedroom windows. Hours of fun (that might eventually lead to arrest, but in the meantime will cheer you up no end).

Overweight and Depressed?

Instead of paying thousands to have your jaw wired up, why not eat in front of a mirror wearing a bikini? You will be so horrified your jaw will drop open and all the food will fall out. This might make a bit of a mess of the carpet, but it'll be worth it in the long run.

Forget that pricey gastric band. Why not go for the non-surgical alternative? Just pop on a pair of your daughter's size-8 knickers. This will be painful and a struggle but really effective, because the elastic biting into your flesh will be a constant reminder that you are a greedy porker and should only be eating celery. Cheap and proven to be medically safe.

Feeling Dissatisfied and Need to Feel Better About Your Lot?

Go on holiday to a really dull Communist state for a fortnight. You'll come back home and experience new-found joy at simple luxuries, such as a shower that works properly, fabric conditioner and cheese that doesn't stink of bleach.

----
* Whistling was more common in the olden days, possibly because songs of the time were easy to whistle – for example, it's much easier to whistle 'Pack Up Your Troubles in Your Old Kitbag' than Dizzee Rascal's 'Bonkers' or anything by Lady Gaga (but that's no reason not to try).

Suffering From Empty-Nest Syndrome?

Visit the zoo with some really naughty under-fives. Or offer to help as a classroom assistant in your local primary school, preferably in the first week of reception class when they need help getting their shoes and coats on and none of them can find the toilet in time. Within two hours you'll have a migraine and if you do have any child-bearing years left, you'll be severely tempted to get your tubes tied.

Feeling Stressed?

Stress can be damaging. It can affect your sleep and your ability to think straight. What you need to do is focus on some mind-numbing but absorbing activity that will take your mind completely off your problems, like playing golf or filling in your tax return. This may of course lead to feelings of defeat and inadequacy, which is progress of some kind, I suppose. Gardening can also be restorative and good for the soul, but it will ruin your nails and lead to some very dull conversations.

Or why not join an outdoor swimming club? This is truly bracing and will either boost your circulation and do you the power of good or will provide the short, sharp shock you need to give you a massive heart attack, which, if you have serious depression, might be the only solution.

Having a 'Slightly Blue' Day?

Chat with a lifelong friend, have a chocolate biscuit (just the one), bake a loaf of bread, sort out a drawer, paint your toenails (but try not to get even more depressed if you can't reach) or have a nice glass of DWW.*

Watch some crap telly. This will cheer you up and make you feel slightly superior. Try: *Coach Party*, *Young, Dumb and Living Off Mum* or *Come Die With Me*.†

After a dose of crap telly, turn it off: watching too much crap telly can actually bring you down and make you feel that life is utterly pointless and what we really need is a big fat meteorite to wipe us all out so that a new, better form of human life can start again from scratch.

The tipping point between being cheered up by crap telly and being

---

* DWW = dry white wine (or, as I call it, lady medicine).

† This spin-off to *Come Dine With Me* is apparently in Channel 4's pipeline. (Ha, ha – joke.)

depressed by it can be quite fine. You might need a few days of experimenting with your dose before you find the right balance. I suggest no more than 60 minutes of crap telly a day. If you have made yourself feel a bit queasy by overdosing on crap telly, it's quite easy to counterbalance the effects by reading a good book.

Other Remedies

A Bit of Culture Popping along to an art gallery is a great idea, particularly if it's free. Not only will you see stuff for nothing, but it's a scientifically proven fact that just one cultural outing a week will release enough of the hormone smugoxedrine to keep you going for another seven days. Smugoxedrine is a really wonderful hormone; it gives you the confidence to talk about yourself and what you've been up to without feeling like a great big fraudulent loser.

Some Exercise We all know that exercise (taken in moderation – just like alcohol) is good for us. Simply going for a short walk can make us feel better (particularly if we walk to the corner shop and buy some chocolate biscuits).

Some Alcohol Ah, booze – guaranteed to make you feel better, unless you have too much, in which case it's guaranteed to make you feel like a weeping sore on the face of the earth. In which case, what you need is...

A Fry-Up Man's culinary reminder to man that life is worth living. Though some people think sex is more important, this is debatable: compare your best-ever shag with your best-ever fry-up. Now, which memory is really making your mouth water? Thought so.

WARNING

The middle classes naturally have slightly raised levels of smugoxedrine. In fact, there is a danger they could suffer from toxic levels should they overload themselves with too much high-brow activity. For this reason, if you're a bit middle-class, we suggest no more than one art-gallery visit, one cinema visit and one music gig/comedy night/theatre trip per week.

CHRISTMAS
MANIFESTO

Right, we really need to get to grips with Christmas. It's got way out of hand and we need to rein it back in. For starters, let's celebrate it on 10 January so we'll be able to do all our shopping in the

sales. That's already saved us a bundle. And if that's too difficult, then let's at least limit the thing: Christmas should start on Christmas Eve and end on Boxing Day. And guess what? This is exactly how it is for men! For women, Christmas begins sometime in October with a list that is going to preoccupy them for the next three months, and ends sometime in June when they've just finished hoovering up the pine needles. So from now on it's a three-day Christmas once every three years. Or only when it snows (not that the global-warming thing seems to be panning out at the moment).

The next thing we need to do is lower everyone's expectations, especially on the food front. Delia or Nigella need to be seen to be total Christmas slobs. We need front-cover photos of Nigella and family gathered round a giant turkey Pot Noodle or of Delia opening a load of Iceland boxes and handing round a turkey TV-dinner platter to her appreciative family. If we set the bar really low, then we've all got a chance of enjoying the damn thing.

Maybe it's time we reinvented the traditional Christmas dinner. Turkey's had its turn; let's choose something cheaper and easier to cook, like shepherd's pie or jam sandwiches.

COME ON, LET'S GIVE MUM A BREAK.

TIPS FOR A
COST-EFFECTIVE CHRISTMAS

✳

Blow any spare meat off the turkey with a hairdryer
(and maybe catch the stray meat in a hairnet).

✳

Forget brandy butter.
No one really needs it; it's disgusting.

✳

Don't buy a fancy new tablecloth to cover up the fact that you've had to squeeze two tables together.
Instead, use a white sheet. Make sure you've washed it, mind, as there are certain stains that might put you off your stuffing.

✳

Go abroad and accuse the airline of losing the suitcase that contained all the presents.

✳

If your children and their friends have nice voices, send them out carol-singing.
Ensure they know the words to at least two decent carols. With any luck they should make enough money to buy a new computer game. With a bit more luck they might accidentally ring Simon Cowell's bell and get signed up to his label. Make sure the ugly kid who does the harmonies hides behind a wall; this is the secret to the success of many bands.

✳

Don't put a glass of port or sherry out for Father Christmas.
He's driving; he can have tap water.

Be prepared for toys that will need batteries.

Bulk-buy a variety of different sizes from the cheap battery stall on the market in advance.

Buy a synthetic tree and a pine-scented air-freshener.

This will fool most people (especially the drunks).

Don't put any coins in the Christmas pud.

Buy your sister a jumper that you like, making sure it's too small for her but just right for you.

Then offer to take it off her hands and tell her you will buy her something else, but somehow never get round to it.

Hide.

A week under the stairs with a tin of Quality Street should see you through the worst of it.

Don't do what a friend of mine did, which was to instruct her husband to mend her hairdryer.

Dutifully he took the hairdryer into the garage, fixed it, pulled a plug out of a nearby socket to test the hairdryer and then went triumphantly back indoors to pronounce the hairdryer fixed. Unfortunately, the plug he had pulled in the garage was connected to a catering-sized freezer where my friend had stashed all her Christmas goodies. Three days later, once the prawns had thawed, she noticed the smell. Over 300 quid's worth of food had gone off and all for the sake of a fifteen-quid hairdryer. Of course, I sympathised, but a bit of me thought it was quite funny.

CHRISTMAS GIFTS

FOR SOME REASON, Christmas has become more about presents than anything else. This is probably because presents are more fun than religion. The original Christmas presents were of course gold, frankincense and myrrh, but considering myrrh and frankincense are a bit tricky to get hold of these days, there's nothing wrong with some nice bath oil and maybe an iTunes voucher.

Christmas is another occasion where we want to lower children's expectations. Kids are greedy and demanding enough without Christmas making them even more greedy and demanding. A lot of this seasonal greed is down to insidious telly advertising, so from now on as soon as the clocks go back at the end of September, we shall put an embargo on advertising children's toys on television. This ban will remain in place until the clocks spring forward in March. We will also ensure that the Christmas Argos catalogue will only be available with a plain brown-paper cover. This will put an end to kids getting hysterical about needing a toy that stores deliberately run out of sometime in November.

Instead of all these toy ads, we can show educational footage of how poor children lived in the olden days – if we force-feed our kids this sort of propaganda throughout the autumn months, by the time they get to Christmas they'll be grateful for a tangerine, a yo-yo and a sugar mouse.

For most of us, buying presents for other people can be a nightmare. It's not just the trauma of spending your precious lunch-hour trailing round the shops trying to find something they won't turn their nose up at, it's also the stupid expense of it all.

STOP! THINK!

GIVING PEOPLE GIFTS DOESN'T HAVE TO MEAN SPENDING MONEY.

AFTER ALL,
IT'S THE THOUGHT THAT COUNTS.

You could, for instance, write these thoughts out on some nice posh paper in gold pen in fancy writing: 'I thought of buying you a convertible Mercedes', or 'I thought of buying you some Jimmy Choo shoes', or 'I thought of buying you a lovely pair of diamond earrings', or 'I thought of buying you that jaunty pair of pink socks you pointed out in the Paul Smith catalogue.'

Or why not push the boat out and actually think about what your loved ones would really like this Christmas? Because the fact is, people don't need more things, especially if they are going to be cheap, rubbish things they don't really want. Why not be more creative? Have you ever thought about writing a poem for your mum, or maybe putting on a Christmas panto?

If you're struggling to come up with a really good poem for your mum, here's one you can copy:

I love you, Mum.
I always have done.
Ever since
I was a bun
In your oven.

Just make sure you copy it out nicely in your best handwriting with no spelling mistakes.

AS WE HAVE ALL BEEN TOLD, IT IS BETTER TO GIVE THAN TO RECEIVE
(UNLESS YOU'VE BOUGHT HIM AN ALFA ROMEO AND HE'S BOUGHT YOU SOME TIGHTS).

Buying presents can be tricky, so much so that a lot of people are opting out of the whole minefield completely and going for charity donations instead. This is all well and good, but after the novelty of owning a goat in Somalia has worn off, people can start to feel a bit bored and restless. What do you do on Christmas Day when you haven't got any new toys to play with? You start drinking, that's what, and very quickly things can turn ugly.

SOME HOMEMADE-GIFT IDEAS

Babies

Make a mobile with coat-hangers and hang things off it, like old CDs you don't listen to any more or some horrible earrings.*

Small children

Make an activity book. This can have colouring-in pages, word searches, maybe a short story (if you can be bothered), some really easy sudokus or a snakes and ladders game.

Twelve-year-olds

A cheap thrill. The only thing twelve-year-old boys want to do is walk through a red-light district and see a live prostitute. This is simple if you live anywhere near London: just catch a bus and walk round the back of Piccadilly. If you don't live near London, take the kid to a local shopping centre, point at some slaggy-looking girls and tell the youngster that they are working girls eating Ginsters pies on their day off.

Teenagers

A free piercing. This can be done anywhere on their body that you can force a needle through. Note: eyebrows can be a bit thick and stiff; ears are loads easier. Tattoos are also a fun idea, but it's illegal to brand a minor, and anyway, their mum will probably kill you. So why not help them apply a fake tattoo to their neck? Not only will they feel cool, but their mother's reaction will make the teenager laugh for years to come.

Students

A dead-cert tip on a horse. This will encourage them to go into a betting shop. With any luck the horse will lose and you will have taught them a valuable life lesson. On the other hand, the horse might win and with those winnings they might go out and buy a load

---

* Make sure when you make this mobile that you attach things properly. Mobiles are often hung directly over a baby's cot and we don't want stuff falling on the baby's face.

of coke. See what you've done? You've ruined their life.

Mums

All mums ever want is a nice time with the family – maybe a nice meal and a nice bottle of wine. Unfortunately, this usually isn't possible, because most families aren't capable of being nice and in the same room simultaneously. So why not make her a pomander?

A pomander can be made by stuffing an orange with cloves and nutmeg. This can then be positioned in a pants drawer in order to delicately scent the underwear with tangy orange and spicy whiffs.

I once got one for my birthday. Unfortunately, the orange went mouldy and some mould spores got into my gussets. No woman needs this kind of trouble.

Dads

Dads get really left out when it comes to presents; they get all the rubbish. This is because all dads really want is expensive stuff like a helicopter, which is silly of them, so they must be punished by getting hankies instead.

There's not much that you can make for the dad who hasn't got much and would really like a yacht, so why not try to do something that's going to make him proud? I know this is tricky, but if possible, you need to save a kid's life or get a first from Oxford. If this isn't an option, then write him a letter promising him one of your kidneys should he ever need it.

Grannies

Grannies are really easy to give homemade presents to – they're grateful for anything in life that conveys love and affection and that they can show off to their friends. Save up all your odd earrings and make them into a collage, or collect seashells and stick them on a box for their dressing table or mantelpiece. (PS This will not work if your granny is the sort of granny who wears heels and winters in Tenerife with her new boyfriend. If this is the case, she won't give a toss whether you give her a present or not, and she isn't a proper granny at all.)

Grandpas

Pull up some plants from your garden or the local park and pot them. Simply tie a pretty bow round the pot and, hey presto, you have a present for a gardening enthusiast. Make up a Latin name for this plant and write it on a homemade label. This will make the gift even more exotic. A friend of mine received a cactus from a garden that once belonged to Salvador Dalí – good story, even if it's bollocks.

HOMEMADE-GIFT IDEAS FOR PEOPLE WITH HOBBIES

It's easier to give presents to people who have hobbies.

Cooks

A lock of Jamie Oliver's hair. As long as it's blond and a bit curly, it won't matter if it's not actually Jamie Oliver's.

Fishermen

A copy of a map with directions to a really good fishing lake in Scotland that is apparently 'rammed with salmon' (doesn't need to be true – remember, it's the thought that counts), plus a Tupperware full of bait (worms) that you have dug up from the garden or some maggots that you have grown yourself by keeping a piece of meat for a bit too long.

Drinkers

Flavour some cheap vodka with some blackcurrant jam – hey presto, blackcurrant vodka. If you're really skint, it's even cheaper to make boozy blackcurrant jam.

Just buy some cheap jam, and once you've used it about twice, top it up with rum or anything you've got knocking around at the back of the cupboard. Now re-label the jar and call it 'Rummy Rumtopf'. Hmm – really nice with ice cream.

Or maybe you could download some information off the Internet about how alcohol is slowly rotting their liver and that if they continue to drink more than the recommended daily amount, then they can expect it to seriously damage their health. This might not be much of a present, especially on Christmas Day, when they are looking forward to getting completely plastered by 11 a.m., but it might be the wake-up call that saves their life. No one could ask for a better gift than that – well done!

The fine art of
OUT-PRESENTING

It might cost you a few quid but that warm smug glow of 'out-presenting' your family (especially your brother and sister) can be quite satisfactory. Imagine the scenario: you've all agreed not to buy each other presents; then, right at the last moment, after a really boring day of no gifts but loads of turkey, you surprise everyone with a suitcase of gaudily wrapped presents for your nearest and dearest. Oh, yes, you win. Even though your mum will be repeating, 'You shouldn't have. You really shouldn't have,' she will secretly be really chuffed that at least one of her ungrateful children has bothered to make the effort. The great thing about out-presenting when no one else has actually bought anything at all is that you don't have to spend much to look like Richard Branson.

WARNING
THIS COULD PUT SUCH A SELF-SATISFIED GRIN ON YOUR FACE YOU RUN THE DANGER OF LOOKING AS SMUG AS RICKY GERVAIS.

Let's Do It Properly

If we are going to celebrate Christmas then let's celebrate properly (no half measures)

CARDS

From now on everyone under 70 must send a minimum of 20 Christmas cards; emails don't count. Well done to those who send personalised Christmas cards – it's good to know who one's pretentious mates are. We'd also like to encourage the writing of round robins, as they make hilarious reading over the Christmas dinner table and are inevitably much funnier than the jokes in the crackers.

LUNCH

That's another thing – while eating our regulation grey Christmas meat – otherwise known as turkey – everyone must wear a paper hat that has fallen out of a cracker. If you're not doing crackers this year, then make your own paper hats.

TELEVISION

Television has a duty at Christmas to entertain the whole family. Unless it delivers, all senior executives should be fired (or forced to watch what they wanted us to watch for an entire year). During the three-day Christmas period, any repeats (apart from certain classic movies and musicals) would be illegal.* It would also be against the law to show any film that has been given away free with a newspaper during the previous twelve months. Wealthy TV channels showing repeats during the festive season is the equivalent of David Beckham giving Victoria some pants that used to belong to Rebecca Loos: it's insulting and unforgivable.

It will also be an offence to schedule the good stuff on one side up against the good stuff on another side. People are a bit too pissed at Christmas to bother recording stuff, so from now on the Christmas schedules will provide variety and choice across all the terrestrial channels.

As well as the soaps and the fashionable sitcoms, there will also be guaranteed Christmas specials of the following: *Wallace and Gromit*, *Come Dine With Me*, *Dr Who*, *Doc Martin*, *Top Gear* and for one day only (Christmas Day) we shall bring back a proper edition of *Top of the Pops*, complete with loads of tinsel and glitter.

FINALLY...

If women have done all the slaving away, cooking, table-setting and serving, then the children and the men must do the clearing, cleaning and tidying up. Local government inspectors will be dispatched to spy through kitchen windows to ensure that this is being done. Any man found snoozing in an armchair before the dining table has been properly cleared will be dragged from said chair and horse-whipped naked in the street – this may or may not be more amusing than last year's *Gavin and Stacey* DVD.

---

* Films that may legally be repeated include: any Alfred Hitchcock; *Whatever Happened to Baby Jane*; *It's a Wonderful Life*; *West Side Story*; *Chicago*; anything starring James McAvoy; any really good Dickens or Jane Austen adaptations; and one of those weird Japanese animated cartoons that end up making you cry.